# Phone Numbers

Mom's work phone: _____ __

Dad's work phone: _____

Neighbor's name: _____

    Phone: _____

Babysitter's name _____

    Phone: _____

School name: _____

    Phone: _____

School name: _____

    Phone: _____


Other phone numbers:

Name: _____

    Phone: _____

Name: _____

    Phone: _____

Name: _____

    Phone: _____

Name: _____

    Phone: _____

Name: _____

    Phone: _____

# What To Do When Your Child Gets Sick

### Gloria Mayer, RN
### Ann Kuklierus, RN

Institute for Healthcare Advancement
(800) 434-4633 • healthliteracysolutions.org

**Library of Congress Cataloging-in-Publication Data**
Mayer, Gloria G.
  What to do when your child gets sick / Gloria Mayer, Ann Kuklierus.
    p. cm.
  Includes index.
  ISBN 978-0-9701245-0-0 (pbk. : alk. paper)
  1. Medical emergencies—Handbooks, manuals, etc. 2. Child care—
Handbooks, manuals, etc. 3. Sick children—Handbooks, manuals, etc.
4. Children—Health and hygiene—Handbooks, manuals, etc. I. Kuklierus,
Ann. II. Title.
  RJ101.M393 2003
  649.8—dc22

                                                        2004010954

Printed in the United States of America.
14 13 12    30 29 28 27

ISBN: 978-0-9701245-0-0

# To Our Readers

This book is for moms, dads, and others who take care of children. We hope this book helps you keep your children safe and well.

## Here are some things to do when you get this book.

- Fill in the phone numbers in the front of this book. Keep this book where it is easy to find.

- Turn to pages 6–10 to find out what's in this book.

- Read and follow the safety tips on pages 12–19.

- See page 5 to find out when to call your doctor.

- Read a few pages of this book every day. This will help you know what to do when your child gets sick.

- Take a class in CPR (cardiopulmonary resuscitation). This will teach you what to do if your child's breathing or heart ever stops, or if your child chokes. Call your local hospital, American Heart Association, or American Red Cross to find out where you can take this class.

- There is a word list at the end of the book. It gives the meaning of some words.

# To Our Readers

This book was read by doctors and nurses trained in caring for children. The doctors and nurses agree with the information in this book. They feel it is safe and helpful.

However, **each child is different.** Some things in this book may not be right for your child. Each mom, dad, or person caring for a child must decide when to call the doctor or when to go to the hospital. If your child is sick and you have doubts, questions, or concerns about advice in this book, call your doctor right away. Always do what your doctor or nurse says.

# When to Call the Doctor or Clinic

Sometimes, you need to call the doctor or get help right away. Here are some of those times:

- Your child has trouble breathing.
- Bleeding will not stop.
- Any injury that you think can lead to your child's death.
- Blood in your child's pee (urine) or BM (bowel movement).
- Coughing up or throwing up blood.
- Diarrhea and no pee (urine) for 6 hours.
- The soft spot on your baby's head is bulging or sunken.
- Pain in the ear or liquid, pus, or blood coming out of your child's ear.
- Your child has a hard time swallowing or won't eat.
- Your child has both a fever and a stiff neck.
- Fever of 100.4 degrees F (rectal), if your baby is younger than 2 months old.
- Fever of 101 degrees F (rectal), if your baby is between 2 and 6 months old.
- Fever of 103 degrees F (rectal), if your baby is between 6 months and 2 years old.

This is a short list of when to call the doctor or get help right away. Read this book for other times to call your doctor or nurse.

# What's in This Book

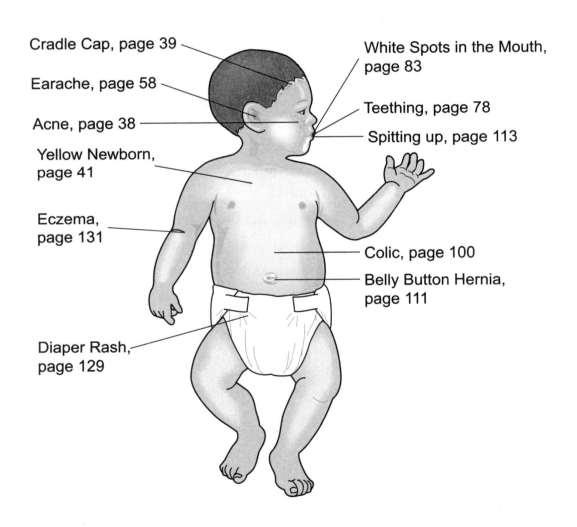

# What's in This Book

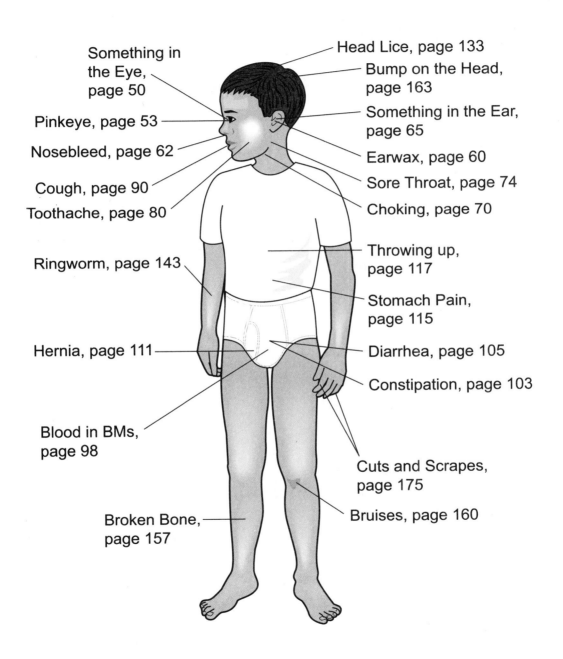

# What's in This Book

# Safety Tips

## 1

**Notes**

_____

_____

_____

_____

_____

_____

_____

_____

_____

_____

_____

_____

_____

_____

_____

_____

# Safety Tips

## What is it?

Safety tips are things to do to keep your child safe.
Many children are badly hurt or die from accidents.
Be wise. Do these things to keep your child safe.

## What can I do to prevent broken bones?

- Never leave a young child alone on a high place even for a few seconds. This includes sofas, changing tables, or shopping carts. Your child can have a bad fall.

- Keep crib rails up to your baby's chin at all times.

- Do not use a baby walker. Your baby can tip over or crash through a safety gate.

- Put safety locks on your windows. Your child can open a window and fall out.

## What can I do to prevent burns?

- Keep matches and lighters away from children. Teach children not to play with matches or other things that can start a fire.

- Put smoke detectors in all bedrooms and the hallway. Test smoke detectors monthly. Put in new batteries every 6 months.

- Get a fire extinguisher for your home. Keep it handy. Know how to use it.

- Teach children to stop, drop to the ground, and roll if their clothes catch on fire.

# Safety Tips

- Set your water heater at 120 degrees F. If it is higher than this, children can be burned by very hot water coming out of the faucet.

- Make sure the bath water isn't too hot before you put your child in the tub. Put your elbow in the bath water to test how hot it is.

- Keep children away from the stove, irons, and curling irons. Turn off and unplug these things when you are not using them.

- Children like to reach up and grab things. Turn pot handles away so your child can't grab them.

- Never hold your child while drinking a hot liquid such as coffee.

- Never hold your child while cooking by the stove.

- Never heat your child's bottle or food in a microwave oven. Some parts may get so hot they can burn your child.

- Teach children what to do in case of a fire.

## What can I do to prevent choking?

- Babies and young children can choke on some foods such as:
  - popcorn
  - peanuts
  - gum
  - grapes
  - hot dogs
  - raisins
  - small hard candy like M&Ms
  - raw vegetables
- Do not give young children anything to eat that is small, hard, and round.
- Children can choke on:
  - balloons
  - cherry pits
  - watch batteries
  - coins
  - orange seeds
- Teach children to chew food well. Cut up foods such as hot dogs, grapes, and raw vegetables into very small pieces.
- Watch children while they eat.
- Do not let your child run with anything in the mouth.
- Check all toys for small parts that can be pulled off.
- Do not give young children toys with parts smaller than this:

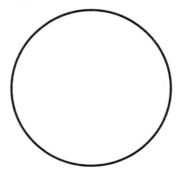

- Check your baby's pacifier every day for cracks and breaks. Buy a new pacifier every 2–3 months.
- Teach your child to put only food in the mouth.

## What can I do to prevent drowning?

- A young child can drown in a very small amount of water, like a pail of water. Do not leave water in pails. Empty baby pools when not in use.

- A young child can also drown in the toilet. Always close the lid and put a latch on it. Lock the bathroom door, or use a safety gate to keep your baby out of the bathroom.

- Never leave your child alone near water. Do not risk it even for a few seconds.

- Do not leave your child alone in the bathtub. Do not risk it even for a few seconds.

- Put fences around pools, spas, ponds, and other bodies of water.

- Teach your child over age 4 how to swim, **but always stay with your child.**
  A child who knows how to swim can still drown.

- Teach your child not to go near water alone.

- Teach your child always to swim with an adult.

## What can I do to prevent head injuries?

- Always put a helmet on your child for certain sports. These include bike riding, rollerblading, skateboarding, and scootering. The helmet should cover the top of your child's forehead.

- Put your child in the back seat of the car. This is the safest place for your child. Always put your child in a car seat or seat belt when driving in the car.

- If you have a passenger air bag, **never** put your child in the front seat.

- Use a car seat until a child is 8 years old, unless they are 4 feet and 9 inches tall or taller.

- The car seat you use depends on your child's age and weight. Read the papers that come with the car seat to make sure it is right for your child.

  - Babies should ride in a rear-facing car seat. Keep babies facing the back of the car until they are over 2 years old and they are bigger than the height and weight for their car seat.

  - Once your child grows out of the rear-facing car seat and is over 2 years old, put him in a toddler car seat that faces the front of the car.

  - There are state laws about when to put a child in a booster seat. Check with your doctor or nurse.

# Safety Tips

- Never leave your child alone in a high place where he or she can fall.
- Keep crib rails up to your baby's chin at all times.
- Place a gate to keep your child away from steps.
- Lock all doors that lead to steps.
- Never shake or hit your baby. Your baby's brain is very soft. A baby can be badly hurt and die from shaking.

## What can I do to prevent poisoning?

- Buy medicines with childproof caps.
- Store medicines and vitamins out of your child's reach.
- If you have people over to your house, ask them if they have any medicines. Put their medicines out of your child's reach.

- Never tell children that medicine is candy.
- Read the label well before giving your child medicine. Many mistakes happen at night. Turn the light on, and take a good look at the label on the bottle.
- Don't give your child someone else's medicine.
- Store all cleaning products and other poisons in locked cabinets. Your child could eat them. Do not keep soap, cleaning products, or anything else under the kitchen or bathroom sink.
- Always keep things in the bottles they came in. Do not put poisons in food jars or bottles.

17

- Don't let your child peel off old paint and eat it. Your child can get lead poisoning.
- Never mix cleaning products together such as bleach and ammonia. It can give off a poison gas that can make you very sick.

## What else can I do to keep my child safe?

- Never leave your child alone in a car. Don't risk it even for a few minutes.
- Put your baby to sleep on his back. Do not put your baby to sleep on the stomach or side. There should be nothing in the crib - no pillows, blankets, toys, or bumper pads.
- Use a baby crib with sides that do not move up and down. There should be no space between the mattress and crib. Make sure the crib bars are less than 2 3/8 inches apart.
- Never put your baby to sleep in your bed. You could roll over on your baby. Do not put your baby to sleep on a sofa, pillow, or soft mattress.
- Do not let your baby wear anything around her neck, such as amber beads or other jewelry.
- Babies and young children like to grab things. Keep your baby's crib away from things your baby can pull into the crib. These include blinds, drapes, and hanging cords.
- Keep all cords out of the reach of children. A child can tie a cord around his neck and die. A child can pull something down by the cord onto his head.

# Safety Tips

- Cover all electric outlets with plastic safety covers.

- Store sharp things away from children. These include knives, needles, pins, and nails.

- Keep plastic bags away from children.

- Cover all sharp corners on furniture.

# Taking Care of Your Sick Child

## 2

Notes

_____
_____
_____
_____
_____
_____
_____
_____
_____
_____
_____
_____
_____
_____
_____
_____
_____
_____

# How to Tell If Your Child Has a Fever

## What is it?

A fever is when the body temperature is hot. The normal temperature of most children is around 98.6 degrees F. To find out if your child has a fever, take your child's temperature. **You must use a thermometer.** Your child may feel warm to the touch, and not have a fever.
If your child has a fever, turn to page 26.

## How do you take a temperature?

There are a few ways to check if your child has a fever. If you are not sure which way to use, ask your doctor or nurse. Never use a glass thermometer to take a temperature.

Here is how to use a digital thermometer. It is safe and easy to use.

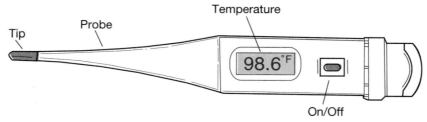

Tip  Probe  Temperature  98.6°F  On/Off

- There are a few types of digital thermometers. Read the paper that comes with the thermometer to learn how to use it. Keep the paper with the thermometer for later use.
- If you don't know how to use the thermometer, ask a nurse or someone at the drugstore.

# How to Tell If Your Child Has a Fever

- A digital thermometer works on a battery. Turn it off when not in use.
- You can use a digital thermometer to take a temperature by:
  - Rectum (rectal)
  - Mouth (oral)
  - Under the arm (axilla)
- This is how you read the temperature.

| | |
|---|---|
| **100.2 °F** | One hundred <u>point</u> two |
| **102 °F** | One hundred <u>and</u> two |

- If you need help to read a thermometer, ask a doctor, nurse, or someone at the drugstore.

**Rectal temperature**

- The best way to check a baby's temperature is rectal.
- You can put a special plastic cover (called a probe cover) over the tip before taking a rectal temperature. If you use a plastic cover, throw it away after each use.
- Put a water soluble jelly such as K-Y jelly on the tip of the thermometer or plastic cover. This makes the thermometer slide into the rectum. **Do not use Vaseline or petroleum jelly.**

- Lay your baby belly-down on your lap.
- For older children, you can use a changing table or a bed.
- Put the tip no more than ½ inch into the rectum. It should slide in easy. Don't push it in.

**———**

½ inch

- Hold the thermometer in place. Hold your child still. Keep your child from rolling onto the thermometer.
- It takes about 1 minute to check a temperature by rectum. The thermometer beeps when it's ready.
- Some thermometers also beep to tell you it is in the right place. Read the paper that comes with the thermometer to know how to use it.
- Wash the tip and probe of the thermometer with soap and warm (not hot) water. Do not put the whole thermometer in water.
- After you use a thermometer to take a rectal temperature, it should not be put in the mouth. You can use it under the arm.

## Mouth (oral) temperature

- Take a temperature by mouth when your child can keep the thermometer under his tongue with his mouth closed.
- Wash the thermometer with soap and warm (not hot) water before using.
- Do not let your child drink anything for 15 minutes. Then take the temperature.
- Put the thermometer under your child's tongue. Have your child close his lips around the thermometer.

- Stay with your child while the thermometer is in your child's mouth. You can hold it in place.

- It takes about 1 minute to check a temperature by mouth. The thermometer beeps when it's ready.

- Your child's temperature shows on the thermometer. See page 23 for how to read the temperature.

**Under the arm (axilla) temperature**

- This way may not give you the right temperature. Tell your doctor if you take your child's temperature this way.

- Read the paper that comes with your thermometer to find out how long to keep it under the arm.

- Use a towel to dry under your child's arm. Then put the tip of the thermometer in the center of the armpit.

- Hold your child's elbow against the body.

- If the temperature is over 100 degrees F, take it again by rectum or mouth.

- See page 23 for how to read the temperature.

## What else should I know about taking a temperature?

- A digital thermometer is not a toy. Keep it out of your child's reach.

- There are other kinds of thermometers. If you don't know which thermometer to use, ask your doctor or nurse.

# Fever

## What is it?

Fever is a body temperature higher than normal. Fever is usually a sign of an illness or infection. The normal temperature of most children is around 98.6 degrees F (oral). The normal range can be from 97.5 to 99 degrees F. Take your child's temperature when he is well. Do this so you will know your child's normal temperature.

## What do I see?

- Your child's face may be red.
- Your child's skin is hot. It may be moist.
- Your child may have the chills.
- His eyes may be glassy.
- Your child's breathing and heartbeat may be fast.
- Your child may be fussy and have a headache.

## What can I do at home?

- Give your child extra fluids to drink. Popsicles and cool drinks help lower fever.
- Dress your child lightly.
- Keep your child's room cool. Turn down the heat. Use a fan if the room is hot.
- Check your child's temperature if your child looks or acts sick.

# Fever

- Give your child acetaminophen or ibuprofen if child is older than 2 years and is fussy or is not eating and drinking well. Read the label to find out how much medicine to give, or ask your doctor or nurse.
- Remove heavy blankets and warm clothes.
- **Do not give aspirin to anyone younger than 21 years.** Aspirin can make a child very sick.
- If your child is vomiting, a rectal suppository may be used. Acetaminophen comes in suppository form. Read the label to use the right suppository for your child's age. Call your doctor if your child is younger than 2 years old.
- If the suppository is too soft, put it in the refrigerator for 10 minutes.
- Take off the wrapper. Put some K-Y jelly on the tip (pointed end). Slide the suppository into the rectum. Use your finger to push it in.
- Wash your hands after.

## When do I call the doctor or nurse?

- Your baby is younger than 6 months and has a fever of 100.4 degrees F or higher.
- Your child is older than 6 months and has a fever of 103 degrees F or higher.
- The fever lasts for more than a day in a child younger than 2 years old.
- Your child has a seizure (convulsion). **Call 911.**
- Your child cries if touched or moved and cannot be comforted.
- Your child has a stiff neck (he cannot touch his chest with his chin) or a bad headache.

- Your child is hard to wake up.
- Your child has a hard time breathing.
- Your baby's soft spot on the head is bulging or sunken.
- Your child has a bad cough, white patches on the throat, burning pee (urine), or ear pain.
- Your child has signs of a skin infection. Some signs are pain, redness, and oozing pus out of the skin.
- Your child has a skin rash.
- Your child throws up (vomits) or has stomach pain or diarrhea.
- Your child has spots that look like bruises.

## What should I do if my child has a seizure (convulsion)?

- Some children, ages to 6 months to 6 years, get seizures from a fever. It is called a febrile seizure. These seizures are usually harmless. But they can be scary for parents.
- A child should see a doctor after a seizure.
- Your child may shake and move his arms and legs. His eyes may roll back.
- Most seizures last 1 or 2 minutes. Some seizures can last up to 15 minutes.
- Place your child on the floor or on a bed.
- **Do not** try to stop arms and legs from moving.

- Turn your child on the side so he or she does not choke on vomit.

- Do not put anything in your child's mouth.

- **Call 911** if:
    - The seizure does not stop in **5** minutes.
    - Your child has trouble breathing
    - Your child is vomiting
    - Your child has a stiff neck

- Put a cold, wet cloth on your child's forehead and neck.

- Do not give your child food or drink during or right after a seizure.

## What else should I know about fever?

- Fever is not an illness. It's the body's response to illness or injury.
- Most fevers are from viral infections. They last 2–3 days.
- Very few children have a seizure from fever.
- Your child can get a fever after getting shots (immunizations). It will be gone in about 24 hours.

# Infection

## What is it?

It is an illness caused by germs that you cannot see.
The germs can spread from one person to another.
Your child can get an infection inside the body
such as a cold or flu. An infection can also be in the skin
such as cuts and scrapes.

## What do I see?

When there is an infection inside
the body, you may see:

- Sneezing and coughing
- Fever
- Pain in the ears, throat, head, or other places
- Burning pee (urine)
- Your child does not want to eat or drink
- Your child looks and acts sick

When there is an infection in the skin, you may see:

- Redness
- Red streaks on the skin near the cut or sore
- Swelling and heat in the skin
- Yellow stuff (pus) oozing out of the cut or sore
- Fever
- Pain

# Infection

## What can I do at home?

- If your doctor orders medicine, be sure your child finishes it all. Do this even if your child looks well after a few days.
- Give your child lots of liquids to drink.
- Wash skin infections well with soap and water.
- Soak the skin. Put medicine on, if your doctor tells you.

## When do I call the doctor or nurse?

- If you think your child has an infection
- If the infection seems to be getting worse

## What can I do to stop the spread of infection?

**Teach your child these things to stop the spread of infection:**

- Wash hands often. Keep hands away from the nose and mouth.
- Cover mouth and nose with a tissue when sneezing and coughing.
- Use clean tissues. Throw tissues away in the trash after using.
- Do not kiss other children or pets.
- Do not use the cups, spoons, or towels of other children.
- Do not touch rashes or sores on other children.

# Infection

**Things you can do to stop the spread of infection:**

- Shots protect your child from certain infections. Make sure your children get all the shots they need.

- Wash your hands well and often.

- Many infections are spread in the kitchen. Use a plastic cutting board. It is hard to get germs off wood boards. Wash the plastic board often with hot water and soap.

- If you have raw meat on a cutting board or counter, wash the area with soap and hot water. Do this before putting any other food on it.

- Cook food well, especially chicken and meat. Cooking kills germs.

- Do not let food that can spoil stay out at room temperature. Store food in the refrigerator.

- Put dirty diapers in closed trash cans.

- Wash toys often using soap and hot water. You can also wash toys with bleach and hot water. Mix 1 ounce of bleach with 8 cups (64 ounces) of hot water.

- Keep your house clean.

# Over-the-Counter Medicines

## What is it?

Over-the-counter medicines are called **OTCs.** They are medicines you can buy in the store without an order (prescription) from your doctor.

## What do I see?

There are many OTCs (over-the-counter medicines). You will only need to use a few for your child. Some OTCs that you should know about are:

- Acetaminophen. Use this for fever or pain.
- Ibuprofen (eye-byoo-PRO-fen). Use this for fever or pain.
- Dimetapp Elixir or PediaCare. Use this for a stuffy or runny nose only if your child is older than 6 years.
- Calamine lotion. Use this for things such as bug bites, on chicken pox sores, and poison ivy.
- Desitin or zinc oxide ointment. Use this for diaper rash.
- Diphenhydramine (die-fen-hie-dra-meen) is the same as Benadryl but costs less. Your doctor or nurse may tell you to give this for allergies, itchy rash, or car sickness.

## What can I do at home?

- Call your doctor before giving OTCs to children younger than 6 years. Diaper rash ointment is OK to use without calling your doctor.

- Give OTCs only when needed. If your child has a fever but is playing and eating, acetaminophen is not needed.

- **Do not give your child aspirin.** Aspirin can make your child very sick. Use acetaminophen instead, or ibuprofen if your child is older than 2 years.

- Always give the correct amount of medicine. Too much medicine can cause poisoning and even death! Read the label very well. If you are not sure how much medicine to give, ask your doctor, nurse, or pharmacist.

- Keep track of when you give your child medicine. This is very important. The best way is to write down the time and amount given.

- Do not give more than 5 doses of acetaminophen in 24 hours.

- Some OTC's such as Dimetapp contain acetaminophen. If you give this medicine, do not give acetaminophen as well.

- Do not wake your child to give an OTC medicine, unless your doctor tells you.

- Always give medicine with the spoon, medicine cup, or dropper that comes with the medicine. If you lose it, ask someone at the drugstore to give you another one.

- **Do not** use a kitchen spoon to measure medicine. You can give too much or too little medicine.

- Do not give medicine by mouth to a child that is throwing up. Do not give it to a sleepy, crying, or coughing child either. Your child can choke on the medicine.

- Do not mix up the words teaspoon and tablespoon.
  The symbol for a teaspoon is a small t.
  The symbol for a tablespoon is a big T.
  There are 3 teaspoons in 1 tablespoon.

  t  = Teaspoon    = Tsp.   = 5 ml. or 5 cc

  T  = Tablespoon  = Tbsp.  = 15 ml. or 15 cc

- Keep all medicines in the bottle they come in.
  Keep all medicines out of the reach of children.

- Do not call medicine "candy."

## When do I call the doctor or nurse?

- Call your doctor before giving OTCs if your child is younger than 6 years.

- You do not know how much medicine to give your child.

- You think your child may be having a reaction to a medicine. Your child may get swelling of the face, body rash, trouble breathing, or vomiting.

- You are worried or have questions.

## What else should I know about OTCs (over-the-counter medicines)?

- Be safe. Read the label well every time you give medicine.

- OTCs will not make your child get well faster. They may make your child feel better.

- If your child has asthma, check with your doctor, nurse, or pharmacist before giving any OTC.

# Your Newborn Baby 3

Notes

# Acne in Newborns

## What is it?

Small white dots on the face. Acne can start at 2–4 weeks of age. It usually goes away when your baby is 4–6 months old.

## What do I see?

- Pimples with dark centers called blackheads.
- Pimples with light centers called whiteheads.
- Pimples are often found on the nose, face, or neck.

## What can I do at home?

- Baby acne will go away on its own over time. Wash your baby's face with a gentle unscented soap.
- Do not pick or scratch the pimples.
- Do not put creams or anything else on pimples.

## When do I call the doctor or nurse?

- Pimples get red or start oozing.

## What else should I know about acne?

- Many babies have pimples that go away around 4–6 months of age. They do not need treatment.
- Pimples do not spread from person to person.

# Cradle Cap

## What is it?

It comes from body oils and old skin that build up on the head. Cradle cap is common in new babies. It looks bad. It does not itch or hurt babies.

## What do I see?

- Yellow, oily crust or scales on your baby's head (scalp).
- Your baby may also have crust on his forehead, in eyebrows, or behind ears.

## What can I do at home?

- Wash your baby's head with baby shampoo.

- While the shampoo is on your baby's head, brush head with a soft brush. This will take off the crust. Comb away scales with a fine-tooth comb. Then rinse her head well.
- If scales are thick, rub baby oil on your baby's head. Wash your baby's head well with shampoo 30 minutes later.
- Some hair may fall out with cradle cap. This is OK. Hair will grow back.

39

# Cradle Cap

## When do I call the doctor or nurse?

- Cradle cap does not go away after 2 weeks of washing and brushing every day.
- Your baby gets a watery rash behind the ears.

## What else should I know about cradle cap?

- Cradle cap can start when your baby is 1 week old.
- It usually goes away within 2 weeks of treatment. It may come back.

# Yellow Newborn (Jaundice)

## What is it?

A new baby's skin and eyes are yellow or orange. A baby can get yellow at 2–4 days old. The yellow should last only 1 week.

## What do I see?

- Your baby's face, chest, stomach, and back look yellow or orange.
- The eyes look yellow.
- Sometimes your baby's arms and legs look yellow or orange.

## What can I do at home?

- Feed your baby every 2–3 hours.
- Make sure your baby has at least 6 wet diapers and a few poops every day.
- Check your baby's color every day in the light from a window. Call your doctor if your baby is getting more yellow or orange.

## When do I call the doctor or nurse?

- Be sure to keep doctor's visit after birth of your baby.
- Your baby gets more yellow or orange, or his arms and legs get yellow or orange.

# Yellow Newborn (Jaundice)

- The yellow or orange color lasts longer than 1 week.
- Your baby has a fever. Turn to page 22 for how to check if your baby has a fever.
- Your baby is sleepy and does not suck well.
- Your baby does not have at least 2 BMs or poops in 24 hours.
- Your baby looks sick.
- Your baby does not have at least 6 wet diapers a day.

# Oozing Belly Button

## What is it?

Liquid coming out from around your baby's belly button (navel).

## What do I see?

- The cord is tied or clamped off. It is still attached to the belly button.

- Skin around the belly button may be red and raw.

- There may be liquid oozing from around the belly button. The liquid may be yellow, green, or bloody.

- Belly button may have a dry crust on or around it.

## What can I do at home?

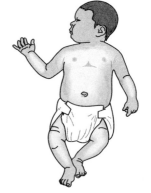

- Keep the belly button dry at all times. Keep the diaper below the belly button. You can cut a V in a throw-away diaper, or you can fold down a cloth diaper.

- Keep the belly button open to the air as much as possible.

- If the belly button gets wet or dirty, clean around the cord with rubbing alcohol on a Q-tip or cotton ball. Use 70% alcohol. You can buy rubbing alcohol at a drugstore or food store.

- Lift the cord and clean right where it meets the body. Do not be afraid. The alcohol does not sting. Baby will cry because the alcohol feels cold.

- Do not get the cord wet until the belly button is all healed. The cord will fall off.

- **Do not** put powder or lotions on or around the belly button.

## When do I call the doctor or nurse?

- The cord is still on at 3 weeks.
- The clamp around the base of the cord comes off.
- Baby has red streaks on the skin around the belly button.
- Baby has a fever.
- There is swelling or redness around the belly button.
- There is a bad smell coming from around the belly button.
- There are pimples or blisters around the belly button.
- Baby has a lot of oozing from around the belly button. The oozing is more than the size of a quarter.
- Baby has bleeding from the belly button that does not stop with pressing.

# Oozing Belly Button

## What else should I know about an oozing belly button?

- A small amount of oozing from around the belly button is normal.

- The cord should fall off in 1–2 weeks.

- Allow the cord to fall off on its own. Do not pull the cord off, even if it is half off.

- Cleaning with rubbing alcohol helps to prevent infection. It also helps the cord to dry and fall off.

- There may be a small amount of bleeding when the cord falls off. The bleeding should not be more than the size of a quarter. It should stop with gentle pressing for 5 minutes.

# Shots (Immunizations)

### What is it?
Shots keep your child from getting bad diseases. Your doctor will decide when to give your baby the first shot.

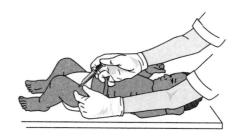

### What do I see?
- Some redness, pain, and swelling where shot was given.
- Your child may cry and be fussy.
- Your child may have a fever and a rash from some shots.

### What can I do at home?
- Have your child rest.
- Ask your doctor if you can give acetaminophen for fever or soreness. Ask how much acetaminophen to give.
- Give your child more liquids to drink.
- A lukewarm bath can help.

### When do I call the doctor or nurse?
- Your child cries for more than 3 hours.
- Your child has a lot of pain where he or she got the shot.
- Your child has a fever for longer than 48 hours.
- Your child looks sick.

# Shots (Immunizations)

- The red area where the shot was given is larger than 2 inches. The redness gets bigger after 24 hours.
- Your child has a seizure (convulsion).
- Your child is sleepy and does not wake up to eat.

## What else should I know about shots?

- Shots are also called vaccinations or immunizations.
- Your child needs to get all the shots to be healthy.
- Your doctor will give you a record of your child's shots. Keep it in a safe place (maybe in this book). You will need it when your child starts school.
- Bring the shot record to each doctor visit.
- Tell your doctor if another clinic gives your child some shots.
- Your doctor may want to give your child other shots or shots at other ages than listed on page 48. This is OK and depends on your child's health and other things. You can check with the County Health Department for more information about shots.

## Shots

- Every child should get immunizations (shots). Shots help keep your child from getting sick.
- Your child may get his/her first shots at the hospital after they are born. Other shots will start later.

# Shots (Immunizations)

- Your child needs shots at or about these ages:
  - 2 Months
  - 4 Months
  - 6 Months
  - 12 Months
  - 15 Months
  - 18 Months
  - 24 Months
  - 4 Years
  - 11 Years
  - 16 Years

- Your doctor or nurse will tell you what shots your child needs and when they should have them. Your doctor may give you a card to bring to every visit, so you have a record of all shots your child has received.

- Always ask your doctor or nurse if your child needs any of these shots:
  - Hepatitis B (HBV)
  - Diphtheria, Tetanus, Pertussis
  - Pneumococcal
  - Flu
  - Varicella
  - Meningococcal
  - Rotavirus
  - Haemophilus influenzae type b
  - Polio
  - Measles, Mumps, Rubella
  - Hepatitis A
  - HPV (Human Papillomavirus)

- The type of shots and the time that children need them change. Always check with your doctor or nurse.

# Your Child's Eyes 4

## Notes

_____

_____

_____

_____

_____

_____

_____

_____

_____

_____

_____

_____

_____

# Something in the Eye

## What is it?

Eyelash, dirt, or other thing or liquid gets into
your child's eye.

## What do I see?

- Eye may be red.
- Your child may not be able to open the eye.
- Your child may have a lot of tears running from the eye.
- Your child quickly opens and closes the eye (blinking).
- Your child may try to rub the eye.
- You may see something in your child's eye.

## What can I do at home?

- Stop your child from rubbing the eye.
- If your child gets a liquid in the
  eye, flush the eye **right away**
  with lots of warm water for
  10–15 minutes. Hold your
  child's eye open under running
  water. You can also flush the
  eye with an eyedropper or cup
  of water.

- Look for something in the corner of the eye.

# Something in the Eye

- Pull down the lower eyelid to look for the thing.

- Check under the upper eyelid by rolling the lid over a Q-tip.

- If you see something, flush the eye with warm water.
- Do not try to remove anything that is stuck in the eye. Cover **both eyes** with a wet washcloth. Call your doctor or go to the hospital.

## When do I call the doctor or nurse?

- Something is stuck in the eye.
- Your child feels there is something in the eye but you can't find it.
- Liquid or blood is coming out of the eye.
- Your child has pain in the eye.
- Your child can't see well 1 hour after the eye was flushed.
- A burning liquid went into your child's eye.
- Vision is suddenly poor.
- Light bothers your child.

## What else should I know about something in the eye?

- Things are often found under the upper lid.
- Rubbing can scratch the eye. It can cause more problems than the thing that got into the eye.
- Both eyes move at the same time. To stop one eye from moving, cover them both.

# Pinkeye

## What is it?

An irritation or infection of the eyes and eyelids. Many things can cause pinkeye. These include allergies, viruses, and bacteria. Pinkeye can spread easily from person to person.

## What do I see?

- The eyes are red. They may have tears.
- Your child may have red, puffy eyelids.
- Your child may have yellow or green crust around the eyes and eyelashes.
- The eyelids may stick together in the morning.
- Your child's eyes may be itchy.

## What can I do at home?

- Wash your hands and your child's hands often.
- Do not let your child rub the eyes.
- Flush eyes with warm running water. Do this if your child gets something in the eyes.

# Pinkeye

- Keep your child's eyes free from crust and pus. Wash the eyes every 1–2 hours while awake. Use warm, wet cotton balls. Use new cotton balls each time.

- Soak off dry crust with warm water. Be careful not to scratch the eyes.

- Put a cool, wet cloth over the eyes to help with itching.

- Do not let your child wear contact lenses or eye make-up.

- Throw away eye make-up used just before pinkeye started. If your child uses the make-up again, the pinkeye can come back.

## What should I do if my doctor orders medicine for pinkeye?

- If your doctor orders eye drops, you may need someone to help you. One person can hold your child, and you can put in the eye drops.

- Tip your child's head back. Gently pull down the lower eyelid to make a cup.

- Put drops in the cup of the eye.

- Have your child gently close the eyes for 2 minutes. This will keep drops in the eye.

- Do not let the eyedropper touch the eye.

- For younger children, have your child lie down and put the drops in the inner corner of the eye. The drops will go into the eye when your child blinks.

- For babies, put drops in while your baby is sleeping.

- Your doctor may order eye ointment instead of drops. Insert a ribbon of ointment from one end of the eye to the other between the lids. Ask your doctor or nurse how to do this.

- Stop using the eye medicine when your child wakes up without any crust in the eyes for 2 mornings.

## When do I call the doctor or nurse?

- Your child's eyes and eyelids are red.

- Your child has pain in the eyes.

- Your child has blurred or loss of vision.

- Your child has yellow or green crust or pus around the eyes.

- The eyes become more red or itchy after medicine is started.

- You think your child may have something in the eye.

- The pupils (black dots in the center of the eyes) are not the same size.

- Your child's friends also have red eyes.

## What else should I know about pinkeye?

- It is easy for pinkeye to spread to other people. Make sure your child washes his or her hands often and does not touch the eyes.

- Your child should not share eye make-up, towels, or washcloths with others.

- Take your child to the doctor if there is yellow or green crust around the eyes. The doctor may order medicine.

# Your Child's Ears and Nose

5

**Notes**

# Earache (Otitis Media)

## What is it?

Pain in the ear caused by liquid or infection. Earaches are common in children. Children often get earaches when they get a cold.

## What do I see?

- Your child pulls or rubs ear.
- Your child screams or cries.
- Your child is fussy and does not want to eat.
- Your child may have a fever.
- Liquid, pus, or blood may leak out of the ear.
- Your child has a hard time sleeping.
- Your child may not hear as well as before.

## What can I do at home?

- Give acetaminophen or ibuprofen for pain and fever, if your child is older than 2 years.
- Give your child more liquids to drink.
- Have your child rest more.
- Be sure to give the medicine the way your doctor tells you.
- Keep all doctor, nurse, or clinic visits, even if your child looks well.

# Earache (Otitis Media)

## When do I call the doctor or nurse?

- Your child has pain in the ear.
- There is liquid, pus, or blood coming out of the ear.
- Your child has a stiff neck or fever.
- Your child is not better after 2–3 days of taking medicine ordered by your doctor.

## What else should I know about earache?

- Breastfeeding your baby may reduce ear infections. Breast milk helps your baby fight germs.
- Give the medicine the way your doctor tells you. Give it for as long as the doctor said, even if your child is better.
- Only use eardrops ordered by your doctor.
- Do not put cotton, Q-tips, or other things into the ear.
- Always feed your baby with the head higher than the shoulders. This will keep milk from going into the ears.
- Do not put your baby to bed with a bottle.
- Put ear medicine in the refrigerator if the label tells you to do so.

# Earwax

## What is it?

It is a thick liquid made by the body to protect the inside of the ear. Earwax is normal. It usually comes out on its own. It can get hard and build up in the ear.

## What do I see?

- Light yellow to dark brown stuff in the ear.
- Your child may not hear as well as before.

## What can I do at home?

- Unless the wax gets hard, no care is needed.
- Wash away wax that comes to the opening of the ear with a damp cloth.
- Do not put Q-tips or other things into your child's ears. This can push the wax farther into the ear.

## What can I do if wax gets hard and stuck in my child's ear?

**Do not do this if your child has ear tubes, an ear infection, or a hole in the eardrum.**

- Put baby oil in small shot glass and place glass in pan of hot water. Test heat of oil on wrist before putting 3–6 drops into your child's ear nightly. Do this for 1–2 weeks.

- Test the oil on your wrist first. It should feel the same temperature as your skin.

- Have your child lay with the ear on a warm heating pad (or warm moist towel) for 20 minutes. This will help melt the wax.

- When the wax is soft enough, it will float out or drain out by itself.

- Turn your child's head so the wax-filled ear is down. This should drain out the oil and wax.

## When do I call the doctor or nurse?

- Your child has pain or bleeding in the ear.
- You can't get hard wax out.
- Your child has ear tubes and may have wax build up.

## What else should I know about earwax?

- Earwax moves to the outside of the ear when your child chews.
- Q-tips should not be used. They can push wax deep into the ear and cause it to get hard and stuck.
- Teach your child to not put anything in the ears.

# Nosebleed

## What is it?

Bleeding in the nose. Nosebleeds are common in children.

## What do I see?

- Blood running out of the nose.
- Your child may spit out or throw up blood that was swallowed.
- Your child may be scared.

## What can I do at home?

- Sit child down and tip head forward. Do not have your child lie down or tilt head back. This will make the blood run into your child's mouth.
- Have your child blow the nose gently.
- Check to see if there is something in the nose.
- Have your child spit out any blood in the mouth.
- Have your child breathe through the mouth.
- Pinch the soft part of the nose for **10 minutes straight.** Do not stop pinching until the 10 minutes is over. If the bleeding does not stop, pinch the nose for another 10 minutes.

# Nosebleed

- Do not stuff anything into your child's nose to stop the bleeding.
- Do not allow your child to pick at or blow the nose for 12 hours after the bleeding stops.

## When do I call the doctor or nurse?

- Your child is younger than 1 year and has a nosebleed.
- Your child has nosebleeds often.
- Your child is bleeding from the mouth or gums.
- Your child is faint, dizzy, or pale and sweaty.
- Your child gets a lot of bruises without falling or getting hurt.

## What else should I know about nosebleeds?

- Nosebleeds often happen when it is hot and dry in the summer. In the winter, the heat may be on in the house and it can be dry and cause nosebleeds. A humidifier may help.
- Blowing or picking the nose can cause nosebleeds.
- If your child has a lot of nosebleeds, ask your doctor about saline nose drops. You can buy it over-the-counter (without a doctor's order).
- It might help to put a few drops of water in your child's nose before blowing.
- A dry nose can bleed. You can put a very small amount of Vaseline in your child's nose. Do this 2 times a day to prevent nosebleeds.

# Nosebleed

- The scab that forms after a nosebleed can be itchy.
  Tell your child not to pick at the scab.
  If it comes off too soon, your child will get
  another nosebleed.

# Something in the Ear

## What is it?

Your child puts a small thing such as a pea into the ear.
A bug can also go into the ear.

## What do I see?

- Your child pulls or rubs the ear.
- Your child may not hear well.
- You may see something in the ear.
- Your child may have pain or feel something in the ear.

## What can I do at home?

### What can I do if my child has a bug in the ear?

- Take your child into a dark room. Shine a light near the outside of the ear. The bug may come out to the light.

- If the bug does not come out, fill the ear with warm baby or olive oil. The bug should float out.

- Turn your child's head so the oil-filled ear is down. This should drain out the oil.

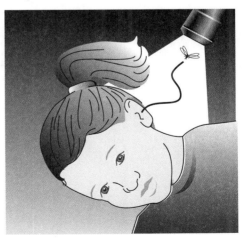

**What can I do if my child has food or something else in the ear?**

- Turn your child's head so the ear with the thing in it is down. Move the ear back and forth. The thing may fall out.

- **Do not** put water in the ear. This can make the thing get bigger and get stuck in the ear.

- **Do not** try to take anything out of the ear with tweezers or a Q-tip. You can push it deeper into the ear.

## When do I call the doctor or nurse?

- You can't get something out of your child's ear.

- Something came out of the ear, but your child has pain.

## What else should I know about something in the ear?

- Children often put small things in their ears.

- Keep small things away from your child.

- Never use something to get an object out of the ear. This can push the thing deeper into the Ear.

# Something in the Nose

## What is it?

Your child puts a small thing or food up the nose.

## What do I see?

- You may see something in the nose.
- There may be a liquid or pus coming out of one or both sides of the nose (nostrils).
  It may be yellow or green and smell bad.
- One or both nostrils may be red and swollen.

## What can I do at home?

- Hold the closed the side of the nose that has nothing in it. Have your child blow through the other side of the nose very hard 3 or 4 times.
- Do not try to take something out of your child's nose using tweezers or your finger. This can push it in more.

## When do I call the doctor or nurse?

- You can see something in the nose, but your child can't blow it out.
- Your child blew something out but now has yellow liquid coming out of the nose.

# Something in the Nose

- A bad-smelling liquid is coming out of your child's nose.
- Your child's nose is red or swollen.
- Your child has a fever.

## What else should I know about something in the nose?

- Children put small things up their nose. These include rice, nuts, beads, candy, and stones.
- Keep small things away from young children.
- Food can get up the nose when your child vomits.

# Your Child's Mouth and Throat

## 6

Notes

_____

_____

_____

_____

_____

_____

_____

_____

_____

_____

_____

_____

_____

_____

_____

_____

_____

# Choking

## What is it?

Food, liquids, or something else blocks your child's throat or airway.

## What do I see?

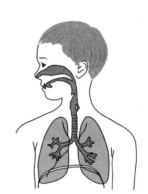

- Your child may cough a lot.
- Your child may not be able to speak, cry, or breathe.
- Your child may turn blue.
- Your child may go limp and pass out.

## What can I do at home?

- Take a Basic Life Support or CPR class. You will learn how to help a child who is choking.
- If your child is coughing, do nothing. Coughing clears the throat and airway. Stay close and watch your child.
- Do not give your child a drink to try to stop the cough.

## What can I do if a child is choking and cannot breathe (the child does not cough, speak, or make a sound)?

### For a baby younger than 1 year old:

- If you are alone, but where others may hear you, shout for help.

70

# Choking

- Hold your baby face down with the head lower than the body.

- Give your baby 5 quick blows to the upper back with the heel of your hand. Hold your baby's head.

- Repeat these steps 5 times. The thing choking your baby should pop out. Take it out of your baby's mouth.

- If it does not pop out (he is limp and not crying), turn your baby over on your lap.

- Place 2 or 3 fingers on the middle of your baby's chest. Push down 5 times until the thing pops out.

- If it does not pop out, look inside your baby's mouth. Take out anything you see. Do not put your fingers in the mouth if you do not see anything.

- If your baby is still not breathing, and help does not come, quickly **call 911. Begin CPR** (turn to page 169).

**For a child older than 1 year who is sitting or standing:**

- If you are alone, but where others may hear you, shout for help.

- Stand behind the child. Put your hands around the child's waist.

- Make a fist with 1 hand. Put the thumb side of your fist on your child's upper stomach, right under the ribs.

- Place your other hand over your fist. Give your child's stomach a quick squeeze.

- Do this until the thing choking your child pops out. Take it out of the mouth.

- If it does not pop out, look inside your child's mouth. Take out anything you see. Do not put your fingers in the mouth if you do not see anything.

- If your child goes limp, and help does not come, **call 911. Begin CPR** (turn to page 169).

**For a child over 1 year old who is on the floor:**

- Turn your child face up.

- Put the heel of 1 hand on your child's upper stomach, right under the ribs.

- Place your other hand on top of the first. Give a quick push into your child's stomach.

- Do this until the thing choking your child pops out. Take it out of the mouth.

- If the thing does not pop out, look inside your child's mouth. Take out anything you see. Do not put your fingers in the mouth if you do not see anything.

- If your child goes limp, and help does not come, **call 911. Begin CPR** (turn to page 169).

**Call 911 if:**

- You cannot get the thing blocking your child's airway out.

- Your child does not start to speak or cry.

- Your child is limp.

# Choking

## What can I do to prevent choking?

- Babies and young children can choke on some foods such as:
  - popcorn
  - peanuts
  - gum
  - grapes
  - hot dogs
  - raisins
  - small hard candy like M&Ms
  - raw vegetables
- Do not give young children anything to eat that is small, hard, and round.
- Children can choke on:
  - balloons
  - cherry pits
  - watch batteries
  - coins
  - orange seeds
- Teach children to chew food well. Cut up foods such as hot dogs, grapes, and raw vegetables into very small pieces.
- Watch children while they eat.
- Do not let your child run with anything in the mouth.
- Check all toys for small parts that can be pulled off.
- Do not give young children toys with parts smaller than this:

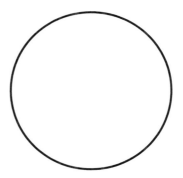

- Check your baby's pacifier every day for cracks and breaks. Buy a new pacifier every 2–3 months.
- Teach your child to put only food in the mouth.

# Sore Throat

## What is it?

Pain in the throat. Most sore throats come with a cold and go away in 3 days.

## What do I see?

- Your child may not want to eat.
- Your child may cry at feeding.
- Your child may have a fever.
- Your child may pull at his ears.
- Her throat is red.
- Her throat may have white or yellow spots.

## What can I do at home?

- Look at your child's throat to see if there are white or yellow spots.
- Give your child soft foods and more liquids to drink. Cold foods help the throat feel better.
- These foods are easy to eat with a sore throat:
  - applesauce
  - ice cream
  - Jell-O
  - popsicles (for child older than 4 years)
- Sodas and citrus juices such as orange juice can hurt the throat.

# Sore Throat

- Give acetaminophen or ibuprofen for pain or fever, if your child is older than 2 years. Ask your doctor how much medicine to give.
- Call your doctor before giving acetaminophen to children younger than 2 years old.
- If your child is younger than 2 months old and has a fever of 100.4 degrees F (rectal) or higher, call your doctor or nurse.
- Children older than 8 years can gargle with mouthwash.
- Some sore throats need medicine. If your doctor orders medicine, be sure to give it the way your doctor tells you.

## When do I call the doctor or nurse?
- Your child has white or yellow spots on the throat.
- Your child can't open the mouth wide.
- Your child is drooling and can't swallow.
- Your child has a hard time breathing.
- Your child will not drink.
- Your child does not pee (urine) in 8 hours.
- Your child also has a rash.

## What else should I know about sore throat?
- Most sore throats do not need medicine.
- Do not use throat sprays sold in stores unless your doctor tells you.
- If your doctor orders medicine, finish it all. Do this even if your child looks well.
- Never give your child old medicine or someone else's medicine.

# Your Child Swallowed Something

### What is it?

Your child swallowed something that isn't food.

### What do I see?

- Something is missing that your child could have swallowed.
- Your child may tell you he swallowed something.
- Your child may choke or cough if something is stuck in the throat.

### What can I do at home?

- If your child looks and feels OK, give him water to drink. If water goes down OK, feed your child some bread.
- Check your child's BMs (bowel movements) every day for the thing swallowed.
- You can cut the BMs with a knife. Or you can strain them with a strainer or a screen.

### When do I call the doctor or nurse?

- Your child swallows:
  - something sharp
  - something larger than a penny

- a watch battery
- more than 1 small magnet
- Your child has trouble swallowing or breathing.
- Your child can't stop coughing or gagging.
- There is blood in your child's BM (bowel movement).
- Your child throws up (vomits) or has stomach pain.
- Your child has pain in the chest or throat.
- Your child looks sick.
- You check your child's BMs for 7 days, and do not find the thing.

## What else should I know about a swallowed thing?

- Most things pass through the body in 3–4 days.
- Keep things away from children that are smaller than this:

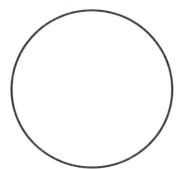

- It is very bad for your child to swallow a watch battery or more than 1 small magnet. Call your doctor right away.

# Teething

## What is it?

New teeth are working their way through the gums. Teething starts when babies are 4–6 months. It can go on until your baby is 2–3 years old.

## What do I see?

- Small bumps on the gums with some redness.
- Gums may be swollen.
- Your baby may be fussy.
- Your baby chews on fingers and puts things in the mouth.
- Your baby's mouth and chin are always wet from drooling.
- Your baby may have blue or black spots on the gums.

## What can I do at home?

- Rub your baby's gums with your finger or a cold wet cloth to help the pain.
- Give your baby a hard (not jell-filled) teething ring, or a cold wet cloth to chew.

## When do I call the doctor or nurse?

- Your baby looks or acts sick.
- You have questions.

## What else should I know about teething?

- Usually medical care is not needed for teething.
- Do not put any teething medicine on gums.

- Do not tie a teething ring around your baby's neck.

- Never put your baby to bed with a bottle or sippy cup of milk or juice. This will rot your baby's teeth.
- Clean your baby's gums and teeth after meals and bedtime with a wet cloth or soft toothbrush.

79

# Toothache

## What is it?

Pain in teeth usually from tooth decay (cavities).

## What do I see?

- You may see white or brown spots on the teeth.
- Your child may have small red bumps on the gum near the tooth.
- Your child may have a swollen cheek.
- Your child may have pus coming out of the gum.
- Your child may have a fever.

## What can I do at home?

- Floss both sides of the tooth. This will remove any stuck food.
- Give acetaminophen for pain, if your child is older than 2 years.

## What can I do to prevent cavities?

- **Do not** put your child to bed with a bottle or sippy cup. The milk or juice sits on the teeth all night. **This may cause cavities.**

- Fluoride fights cavities. Most tap water has fluoride. Ask your doctor if your child needs to take more fluoride.

- Begin cleaning your baby's teeth every day as soon as they appear. Use a small soft toothbrush or wet cloth. You don't need toothpaste. If you use toothpaste, use a small amount. For a child younger than 3 years old, use a smear. For children from 3–6 years old use a small amount, the size of a pea. Your child must be able to spit out the toothpaste.

- Begin to teach your child to brush teeth at 2 years old. You need to help your child brush until 6 years old.

- See a dentist when your child gets the first tooth and not later than 1 year of age.

- Teach your child to floss at an early age. Start as soon as your child has teeth that touch each other.

- Help your child with tooth care until she is 6 years old.

- Buy a new toothbrush every 3–4 months. Everyone in the family needs their own toothbrush. A toothbrush should not be shared.

## When do I call the doctor, nurse, or dentist?

- Call your dentist if you see a brown or black spot in the mouth.

- Call your dentist if your child has tooth pain.

- Call your doctor if your child has a fever or swelling in the cheek, jaw, or chin.

## What else should I know about teeth and a toothache?

- Your child's teeth are very important. Take good care of them.

- All tooth cavities should be seen by a dentist.

- Tooth sealant is a clear cover put on teeth to stop decay. Ask your dentist about sealants.

- Toothpaste has fluoride. Use only a little bit, no more than the size of a pea, when brushing your child's teeth. Do not let your child eat toothpaste.

- Some children like to eat toothpaste. Keep toothpaste out of your child's reach.

- Your child needs to spit out toothpaste.

# White Spots in the Mouth (Thrush)

## What is it?

Thrush is an infection in the mouth.

## What do I see?

- White spots that look like milk on your baby's tongue, gums, and inside lips and cheeks.
- If you rub the white spots, they do not come off.
- Your baby may cry while sucking.

## What can I do at home?

- Your baby needs medicine from the doctor.
- Give your baby medicine after meals.
- Put medicine on the inside of each cheek. You can rub the medicine on the spots with your finger. Be sure to wash your hands well before you do this.

- Do not give your baby food or drink for 30 minutes after the medicine is given.
- Feed your baby with a cup or spoon if your baby can't suck.
- Use a clean nipple with each feeding.

- Always use clean bottles for a feeding.
  Do not reuse milk bottles that are not washed.
- Wash everything your baby puts in the mouth with soap and hot water.
- Replace nipples and pacifier after treatment. Or clean them by putting them in boiling water for 5 minutes.

## When do I call the doctor or nurse?

- Your baby has white spots in the mouth. They do not come off with gentle rubbing.
- Your baby does not want to eat.
- Spots do not go away in 10 days with medicine.
- Your baby has a fever of over 100 degrees F (rectal).
- Your baby also has a diaper rash.

## What else should I know about thrush?

- Do not put your baby to bed with a bottle or pacifier.

- Always wash pacifiers and nipples well with soap and hot water.
- Always wash your hands well before feeding your baby.
- Call your doctor if you are breastfeeding, and you get pain, itch, or pink flaky skin on your nipples.
- Your baby can also get thrush in the diaper area.

# Your Child's Breathing 7

# Cold and Flu

## What is it?

An easily spread illness (virus) of the nose and throat. It lasts about 7 days. Children get about 6 colds a year.

## What do I see?

- Red, runny nose
- Sneezing
- Watery eyes
- Cough
- Your child does not want to eat
- Your baby has trouble drinking from bottle or breast
- Fever and chills

## What can I do at home?

- The best way to protect your child from the flu is with a flu shot. Everyone in the family over the age of 6 months should get a flu shot every year.
- Have your child get a lot of rest.
- Raise your child's head when he is sleeping. This will help breathing. Raise your baby's head by putting something under the mattress. Never put a pillow in a baby's bed.
- Give your child liquids to drink every hour while she is awake.

- Use tissues only once and then throw them away.

- Give acetaminophen or ibuprofen for pain or fever, if your child is older than 2 years. Ask your doctor how much medicine to give.

- Call your doctor before giving acetaminophen to children between 6 months and 2 years. Do not give acetaminophen to babies younger than 6 months. See Fever pages 26–29.

- If your child is younger than 2 months old and has a fever of 100.4 degrees F, call your doctor or nurse.

- Sometimes babies cannot suck because of a stuffed nose. You can use a soft rubber suction bulb to clear a stuffed nose. This will help your baby suck.

- Normal saline nose drops in the nose can help clear nasal mucus.

## How do I use a suction bulb?

- Squeeze the bulb first to push the air out.

- Gently put the rubber tip into one side of your baby's nose (nostril).

- Slowly stop squeezing the bulb.

- This will suck the liquid out of your baby's nose.

- Empty the liquid into the trash.

- Repeat this for the other nostril.

- Do not do this more than 3–4 times a day.

- After using, wash the suction bulb with soap and warm water.

## When do I call the doctor or nurse?

- Your baby is 2 months or younger and shows signs of a cold or the flu.

- See a doctor right away or go to the emergency room if your baby is 2 months or younger and has a fever of 100.4 degrees F.

- Breathing is still hard after the nose is cleaned with a suction bulb.

- Your child has neck pain or a stiff neck.

- Your child has ear pain.

- Your child has a rash or red sores on the skin.

- Your child coughs up green, yellow, or gray stuff.

- Your child looks or acts sick.

- Your child has a fever of over 100.4 degrees F for more than 3 days.

- Your child has trouble swallowing.

- Your child does not drink much. He or she pees only small amounts or less than once every 6 hours.

- Your baby won't stop crying.

- Your baby is sleepy and won't eat or drink.

- Your baby does not have at least 6 wet diapers a day.

## What else should I know about cold and flu?

- The flu is a serious illness for young children. The best way to protect them is with a flu shot.

- There is no medicine to cure a cold or the flu. Your child will get better with time, rest, and lots of liquids.

# Cold and Flu

- A cold or the flu can lead to other sickness. Call your doctor if your child is not better in 7 days.

- Colds and the flu pass from one person to another easily. Use clean tissues to cover coughs and sneezes. Wash your hands after.

- Teach your child to wash his hands often.

# Cough

## What is it?

It's the body's way of clearing the throat, airway, and lungs. A cough is not an illness. It can be a sign of illness.

## What do I see?

- Your child may bring up clear, white, yellow, green, or brown mucus with cough.
- Your child may be unable to sleep due to cough.
- Your child may cough non-stop (coughing spasm).
- Your child may have a hard time breathing when coughing.
- Your child may have a fever.
- Your child may have a runny stuffed nose.

## What can I do at home?

- Give your child lots of liquids to drink. Warm lemonade, apple juice, and water are good.
- Dry air can make your child cough more. Run a cool or warm mist humidifier in your child's room at night. Steam from a shower can also help a dry cough.

- Smoke in the air can make a child cough. Never let anyone smoke around your child.

- You can use honey to quiet a cough for children older than 1 year. **Do not** give honey to babies younger than 1 year.

- If your child has trouble sleeping because of a dry cough, ask your doctor or nurse if you should give him cough medicine. Ask your doctor or pharmacist to help you choose the right medicine.

- If your child has a wet cough, do not give over-the-counter cough medicine unless your doctor tells you. A wet cough means your child brings up mucus when he or she coughs.

## When do I call the doctor or nurse?

- Call your doctor before giving OTCs (over-the-counter medicine) if your child is younger than 6 years.

- A baby younger than 3 months has a cough.

- Your child coughs up blood.

- Your child's lips turn blue when she coughs.

- Breathing is fast and hard.

- Your child cannot breathe. **Call 911.**

- Your child wheezes (makes a whistling sound) or a barking sound.

- Coughing starts after your child chokes on food.

- Your child coughs up thick green or brown mucus.

- Your child cannot stop coughing.

- Your child has pain in the chest from coughing.

- Your child has a fever for more than 3 days with a cough.

- Your child throws up (vomits) while coughing.

- Cough lasts for longer than 7 days.
- Your child cannot sleep due to coughing.

## What else should I know about cough?

- Many things can cause a cough. These include smoke, allergies, and viral infections.
- Do not let anyone smoke around your child. The smoke in the air is called secondhand smoke. It is very bad for your child to breathe secondhand smoke.
- Do not give your child cough medicine during the day, unless your doctor tells you.
- The cough will get better as the illness gets better.

# Croup Cough

## What is it?

A child has a hard time breathing. He has a cough that sounds like the bark of a dog or seal. Croup often gets worse at night. It can start suddenly.

## What do I see?

- Your child has trouble breathing.
- Your child may have noisy breathing.
- Your child may be drooling.
- Your child may be scared.
- Your child may have a fever.
- His nostrils may flare when your child breathes in.
- Spaces between ribs may be sucked in when your child breathes in.
- Your child may not be able to talk or cry due to hard breathing.

## What can I do at home?

- Run a cool mist humidifier next to your child's bed for 1 week. Dress him warmly. Keep the room cool.

- Fill the bathroom with steam by running hot water with the door closed. Sit in the bathroom with your child for 20 minutes. Read a story out loud to calm your child.

- Breathing also can get better with cool moist air. You can wrap your child in a blanket and go out in the night air for 10–20 minutes.

- You may have to repeat these things a few times during the night, if your child wakes up.

- Give your child warm, clear liquids. Apple juice, water, and tea are good. They will loosen mucus and relax the throat.

- **Do not give your child any cough medicine.** Cough medicine does not help this kind of cough.

- Do not allow anyone to smoke around your child.

## When do I call the doctor or nurse?

- **Call 911** if child stops breathing or turns blue. **Start CPR** (turn to page 169).

- Your child makes a squeaky sound breathing in.

- If your child makes a squeaky sound breathing out, call your doctor. Your child may have asthma.

- Your child is drooling and can't talk or swallow.

- Breathing is so hard that your child cannot walk.

- Your child is not better after going out in the night air or with bathroom steam.
- Your child coughs non-stop for 1 hour.
- Croup happens more than 3 nights in a row.
- Croup does not get better in the daytime.
- Croup starts after your child is bitten by a bug or takes medicine. **Call 911.**
- Your child has ear pain and a bad sore throat.

## What else should I know about croup?

- Croup is caused by a virus. It is more common in children 2–4 years old.
- Croup can happen every night for 7 nights. Watch your child closely for trouble breathing.

# Your Child's Stomach 8

Notes

# Blood in BMs
# (Bowel Movements)

## What is it?
There is blood in your child's BM.
BM is also called a bowel movement or stool.

## What do I see?
- Bright red blood on the BM.
- The toilet water may turn red.
- There is blood on the toilet paper or wipes.
- The BM may be black or very dark red.
- Your child may have diarrhea.
- Your child may look sick.

## What can I do at home?
- Look for small cuts on your child's rectum. This can happen if your child is constipated (if the BMs are dry and hard).
- Watch the color of the BMs. Take a sample for the doctor to see.
- Do not give red foods or red drinks to your child.

# Blood in BMs (Bowel Movements)

## When do I call the doctor or nurse?

- The BMs are black or red.
- You think your child has blood in the BMs.

## What else should I know about blood in the BM?

- Red food or red drink in the past 24 hours can cause red BMs. It may not be blood.
- BMs may turn black if your child swallowed blood after a nosebleed. Black foods such as Oreo cookies can also make BMs black.
- BMs can have some blood on the outside if your child has a sore or a small cut in the rectum.
- Some medicines, such as vitamins, have iron. This can make BMs black.
- Normal BMs are yellow, green, light brown, or dark brown.

# Colic

## What is it?

Your baby cries for 3 hours or more, more than 3–4 times a week, and nothing you do seems to help. Colic is very common. Crying spells may begin at 2 weeks of age. Colic often stops when a baby is 3–4 months, but it can last longer.

## What do I see?

- Your baby cries for no reason.
- Your baby is fine when not crying.
- Crying spells can happen 3–4 times a week and last 3–4 hours.
- Your baby may pull his legs up to the belly while crying. He may also hold his legs straight out during crying spells.

## What can I do at home?

- Gently hold and rock your baby.
- Try putting your baby in a baby swing.
- Take your baby for a walk in the stroller.

# Colic

- Try wrapping your baby snugly in a blanket.
- Give your baby a nipple called a pacifier.

- Burp your baby a lot or after every ½ ounce of breast milk or formula.
- Find out what works best for your baby and then do that.
- Get someone to help you care for your baby when you need a break.
- Do not give any medicine to your baby unless your doctor tells you.

## When do I call the doctor or nurse?

- Your baby cries longer than usual.
- Your baby seems to be in pain when crying.
- Your baby acts sick when not crying.
- Your baby has crying spells after 4 months old.
- Your baby has a fever.
- Your baby is not eating.
- You are worried.
- You think something may be wrong.

## What else should I know about colic?

- Colic is not a sign that you are a bad parent or doing something wrong.

- Talk to other moms and dads. Learn what they do for a crying baby.

- Do not yell or hit your baby. Just hold and rock him.

- Never shake your baby. A baby can be badly hurt and die from shaking.

- You may feel tired or bad, because you don't know what to do. Put your baby in a safe place for 10 minutes and walk away. Call someone to help you so you can take a break.

## What other things can I do to calm a crying baby?

- Take your baby for a ride in the car.

- Turn on the vacuum cleaner or the clothes dryer.

- Play soft music or turn on the TV.

# Constipation

## What is it?

Hard, dry BMs (bowel movements) that are painful to pass.

## What do I see?

- Your child has BMs less often than before.
- He cannot have a BM even after trying many times.
- The BM is very hard when it finally comes out.

## What can I do at home?

- Give your child lots of liquids to drink.
- If extra water doesn't work and your baby is younger than 1 year, give 1–2 ounces of prune juice mixed with water (half prune juice and half water) twice a day.
- For babies older than 6 months, feed these foods twice a day:
  - peas
  - beans
  - pears
  - plums
  - prunes
  - sweet potatoes
  - peaches
- For babies older than 1 year, give these foods:
  - peas
  - beans
  - prunes
  - dates
  - apple juice
  - graham crackers
  - bran cereal
  - bran muffins
  - whole wheat bread

# Constipation

- Help your child become more active. Have him walk, run, and play more.

- Stop giving these foods until BMs are regular:
  - ice cream
  - rice
  - carrots
  - cheese
  - bananas
- Do not give medicine for constipation unless your doctor tells you.

## When do I call the doctor or nurse?

- Your child has belly (stomach) pains.
- A BM looks black.
- You see blood on the BM.
- You see brown liquid in your potty-trained child's pants before or after a BM.
- Your child has not had a BM for 3 days after you try home care.

## What else should I know about constipation?

- Do not put any medicine in your child's bottom unless your doctor tells you.
- Your baby may get red in the face, grunt, and strain when having a BM. If a BM is soft when it comes out, this can be normal.
- Some babies can go 2–3 days without having a BM. This can be normal. Children do not need to have a BM everyday.

# Diarrhea

## What is it?

There are many watery or very soft BMs (bowel movements). Your child can get diarrhea with a cold, the flu, or other sickness. Diarrhea is sometimes called "having the runs."

## What do I see?

- More BMs than before.
- BMs are more watery.
- Your child's bottom may be red and sore.
- Your child may have a fever.
- Your child may have pain in the belly (stomach).

## What can I do at home?

- If you are breastfeeding, you should continue.
- If your baby on formula has more than 4 watery BMs a day, check with your doctor or nurse if you should stop the formula for 24 hours.
- Give your baby clear liquids such as Pedialyte.
- Children on solid food, who take clear liquids well and are hungry, can eat small amounts of these foods:
  - mashed ripe bananas
  - applesauce
  - rice cereal
  - dry toast

- When diarrhea stops, slowly begin to feed your child regular foods. Give milk or formula 24–48 hours after diarrhea stops.

- Diarrhea burns the skin. Change your baby's diaper right after each BM. Wash your baby's bottom with mild soap and water. Cover his bottom with Desitin or zinc oxide ointment to prevent diaper rash.

- Do not use baby wipes for diarrhea. Baby wipes can burn her skin.

- Help older children to clean their bottoms to prevent sore bottoms. Give your child tub baths.

- Do not give your child any over-the-counter medicine (OTC) for diarrhea without asking your doctor.

## When do I call the doctor or nurse?

- Your child looks and acts sick.

- Your child does not drink any liquids.

- Little or no pee (urine) in 6–8 hours.

- Your child's mouth looks dry and sticky.

- Your child has other signs of dehydration (see page 107).

- Your child has a fever.

- You see blood in your child's BMs.

- Your child has bad pain in the belly (stomach).

## What can I do to prevent diarrhea?

- Germs cause diarrhea. Always wash your hands after changing a diaper.

- Wash your baby's hands often. Teach children to wash their hands before eating and after using the bathroom.

- Wash your baby's bottles and nipples with soap and very hot water. Rinse well.
- Throw away formula that your baby did not drink. Do not use it later.
- Germs grow on food at room temperature. Store all food that can spoil in the refrigerator.

## What else should I know about diarrhea?

- Diarrhea can be bad because your child can lose a lot of water from the body. This is called dehydration. Call your doctor right away if your child has **any** of these signs.
- Signs of dehydration are:
  - Dry mouth
  - Sunken eyes
  - Little or no pee (urine) in 6 hours
  - Pee is dark yellow.
  - Crying with no tears
  - The soft spot on top of your baby's head is sunken
- New babies have many BMs. This is OK.
- Breastfed babies can have a BM with and after every feeding.
- Breastfed babies have diarrhea less often. Breast milk does not have germs that can cause diarrhea. Breast milk helps babies fight infection.
- Bottle-fed babies can have 1–8 BMs a day during the first week. Then they can have 1–4 BMs until they are 2 months old.
- Babies older than 2 months can have 1–2 BMs a day.

# Food Allergies

## What is it?

Your child eats food that makes him sick every time.

## What do I see?

- Your child's lips, tongue, or mouth can get puffy or swell.
- Your child may have diarrhea or vomiting.
- Your child may have a red rash all over the body.
- Your child may have a hard time breathing.
- Your child may have a sore throat or a runny nose.

## What can I do at home?

- If you know the food that makes your child sick, do not feed it to her.
- Read labels to find out what things are in your child's food. If the food has anything that makes him sick, don't feed it to him.
- If you do not know what makes your child sick, keep a list of all the foods she eats. See which ones have a bad effect.
- When starting new foods, give your baby 1 new food at a time. Feed your baby a lot of this new food. See if your baby gets sick after eating it. Wait 3 days before giving your baby another new food.

- If your child eats many foods and 1 food makes him sick, stop 1 food at a time. Stop feeding 1 food for a week, and see how your child feels.

## When do I call the doctor or nurse?

- Your child cannot breathe, turns blue or white, or has chest pain after eating. **Call 911.**
- Your child's face, neck, lips, or mouth gets bigger. **Call 911.**
- Your child gets sick from many foods.
- You think your baby may be allergic to formula.

## What else should I know about food allergies?

- Breastfed babies have fewer problems with allergies.
- When children are allergic to food, they may get sicker **every time** they eat it. Find out which foods make your child sick. Stop giving this food to your child.
- By the age of 2 or 3, many children can eat foods that once made them sick. But some children get sick from the same foods all their life.
- Common foods that can give children allergies:
  - eggs
  - soybeans
  - wheat
  - chocolate
  - citrus juice or fruit such as oranges
  - fish
  - cow's milk
  - peanuts/peanut butter
  - corn
  - strawberries
  - shellfish such as shrimp, crab
  - nuts

- Check with your doctor before giving babies younger than 1 year shellfish, egg whites, strawberries, and chocolate.

- Tell everyone who takes care of your child about your child's food allergies. Let them know what foods are OK. Give them a list of foods your child can't eat.

- Be sure to tell the daycare or school about your child's allergies.

- When your child goes to a party, be sure to tell the adult what food your child can't eat.

- Before ordering meals at a restaurant, ask how foods are made. Find out what foods are in a meal, such as eggs used to make a sauce.

- Get a medical alert bracelet if your child's food allergies are very bad. Your child wears the bracelet all the time. It tells about your child's food allergies. Ask your doctor or nurse if you should get a bracelet for your child.

- Ask your doctor if you can give your child an over-the-counter medicine such as Benadryl for a mild reaction. Ask how much medicine to give.

- Ask your doctor if your child needs an EpiPen. It is an injection you give for a very bad allergic reaction.

- Teach older children what foods they shouldn't eat.

# Hernia

## What is it?

A popping out or bulging in the groin area or belly button.

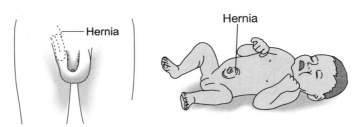

## What do I see?

- A lump in the groin or belly button.
- The lump may show up when your baby cries. It can go away when your baby stops crying.
- The skin over the lump may turn red.

## What can I do at home?

- Watch for lumps and tell your doctor if you see one.

## When do I call the doctor or nurse?

- Call your doctor right away if your child has a lump and pain, fever, or vomits.
- Call your doctor right away if the skin over the lump turns red or blue.
- Let the doctor know about any lump. Do this even if the lump goes away when your baby stops crying.

## What else should I know about a hernia?

- More boys than girls get hernias.

- Some hernias are not bad. Other hernias can be very bad. Get your child to a doctor right away if he or she has pain, fever, or vomits.

- A hernia around a baby's belly button is OK, if it is smaller than a quarter.
  It will go away after your baby learns to walk.

- Do not put anything tight around a belly button hernia. It can make your baby very sick.

# Spitting Up

## What is it?

Right after feeding, your baby brings up 1 or 2 mouthfuls of milk or liquid from the stomach. Many babies spit up after feeding. Spit up can happen with a burp.

## What do I see?

- A small amount of feeding runs out of your baby's mouth.
- Your baby may want to eat after spitting up.

## What can I do at home?

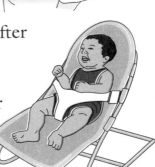

- Feed your baby smaller amounts.
- Wait 2½ hours between feedings so your baby's stomach can empty.
- Burp your baby after every ½ ounce of breast milk or formula.
- Do not press on your baby's stomach after feeding.
- Keep your baby quiet during and after feedings. Keep your baby's head higher than the stomach.
- Hold your baby upright after a feeding. If you have to put your baby down, put him in a baby seat.
- Do not put the diaper on too tight around the stomach.

**113**

## When do I call the doctor or nurse?
- There is blood in spit up.
- Your baby chokes or coughs with spit up.
- Your baby spits up a lot and is not gaining weight.
- Your baby's spit up lands several feet away from him.
- Spit up happens more often and gets more forceful.

## What else should I know about spitting up?
- Feeding your baby too much at one time can cause spit up.
- Holding your baby's legs up to the chest while changing her diaper can cause spit up.
- Spitting up is not vomiting. Spit up happens right after a feeding. It is a small amount of liquid, and it comes out like drooling.
- Spit up stops or gets less when your baby is 10–12 months old.
- Breastfed babies may spit up less than formula-fed babies.
- Soak stains from spit up in baking soda and water. Breast milk does not stain clothes.

# Stomach Pain

## What is it?
Your child complains that her stomach hurts.

## What do I see?
- Your child may lie down and hold her stomach.
- Your child may bring knees up to the stomach.
- Your child may cry or scream with pain.
- Your child may throw up.
- Your child may have diarrhea.

## What can I do at home?
- **Do not** give your child anything to eat or drink until the pain has gone.
- Have your child lie down. Help your child to relax by taking deep breaths.
- Put a warm cloth or heating pad on your child's stomach.
- **Do not** give your child any medicine for the pain.

## When do I call the doctor or nurse?
- Your child is younger than 2 years old and has stomach pain.
- Your child has bad pain and will not stop crying.
- Your child walks bent over, holding his stomach.

- Your child lies down and refuses to walk.
- Your child has pain in lower right side of the stomach for more than 2 hours.
- There is blood in your child's BMs.
- Stomach pains come and go for 12 hours. The pain is not from vomiting or diarrhea.
- Your child got hurt in the stomach.
- Your child's stomach is hard and sore when you touch it.
- Your child has a fever and bad pain.
- Your child has very little pee (urine).
- Your child has a BM that looks like **currant jelly**.

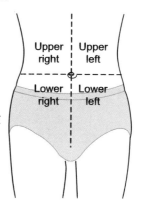

## What else should I know about stomach pain?

- Stomach pain often goes away in less than 2 hours.
- Stomach pain can come from many things such as:
  - flu
  - worry
  - constipation
  - eating too much
  - spoiled food

# Throwing Up (Vomiting)

## What is it?

Your child brings up liquid from the stomach and spits it out.

## What do I see?

- Vomit may have bits of food in it or just stomach liquid.
- Your child may have a fever.
- Your child may have diarrhea.
- Your child may have stomach pains.

## What can I do at home?

- Put a basin next to your child and tie her hair back.
- After your child vomits, help your child to brush his teeth. This helps get the bad taste out of the mouth.
- Do not give your child anything to eat or drink for 2 hours after vomiting.

### For a child 1 year or older:

- After 2 hours of not throwing up, give small amounts of clear drinks. These drinks include Pedialyte, Infalyte, or a store brand of these. Give 1 tablespoon every 3–5 minutes. For older children, give 7-Up that has no bubbles (let it sit open for 2 hours), Jell-O, Gatorade, and Popsicles. If your child does not throw up, double the amount given every hour.

- If your child does not throw up after 4 hours, you can give him or her more to drink.

- Start soft foods after 8 hours of no vomiting. Soft foods include dry toast, rice, bananas, applesauce, and mashed potatoes.

- If your child does not throw up for a day after eating soft foods, give him the usual foods. Stay away from meat, milk, and greasy foods for a few days.

**For a baby younger than 1 year old:**
- If you are breastfeeding, don't stop. Add a bottle of special baby water called Pedialyte, Infalyte or a store brand of these.

- If your baby is bottle-fed, stop formula. Instead give your baby special water called Pedialyte, Infalyte or a store brand of these.

- Start formula 3–4 hours after your baby stops vomiting.

- Return to usual foods in 1 day.

## When do I call the doctor or nurse?
- Your baby is 3 months old or younger and is throwing up.
- Your child does not pee in 6 hours.
- Your child cries with no tears.
- There is blood in the throw-up.
- Your child has bad stomach pain.

# Throwing Up (Vomiting)

- Your child vomits after getting hit on the head or in the stomach.
- Your child vomits after an accident.
- Your child looks very sick.
- Your child has a bad headache.
- Your child cannot keep any liquids in the stomach.

## What else should I know about vomiting?

- Babies often spit up small amounts during or after feeding (see page 113). This is not vomiting.
- Vomiting may be part of another sickness.
- Vomiting can cause your child to lose a lot of water from the body. This is called dehydration. Call your doctor right away if your child has **any** of these signs.
- Signs of dehydration are:
    - Dry mouth
    - Sunken eyes
    - Little or no pee (urine) in 6 hours
    - Pee is dark yellow.
    - Crying with no tears
    - The soft spot on top of your baby's head is sunken.
- Don't give your child red liquids or food. If you do, vomit can look like blood.
- If your baby throws up with force, vomit can come out the nose. You can clear the nose with a suction bulb (see page 87).

# Bed-Wetting

9

# Bed-Wetting

## What is it?
The child is dry during the day, but he pees in bed while sleeping. Many children wet the bed at night. They do not wake up from an urge to pee.

## What do I see?
Wet bed in the morning or in the middle of the night.

## What can I do at home?
- Do not give your child drinks with caffeine or sugar such as sodas.
- Do not give your child anything to drink 2–3 hours before bed.
- Have your child pee right before going to bed.
- Set an alarm to wake your child up 1–2 times during the night to go to the bathroom.
- Put plastic under the sheets to protect the mattress.
- Leave a light on in the bathroom.
- Try a potty-chair next to your child's bed.

- Do not get angry or make fun of your child. Your child does not want to wet the bed.

- Praise your child for dry nights.

- Do not put diapers on your child unless she wants to wear diapers.

## When do I call the doctor or nurse?

- Your child has a fever or stomach pain.

- Your child starts to wet himself during the day.

- Your child has pain or burning when peeing.

- There is blood in your child's pee.

- Your child wants to drink more fluids than before.

- Your child still wets the bed at age 8.

- You would like to know about bed-wetting alarms. These alarms wake children up when they start to wet the bed.

- Your child has been dry at night for 6 months or more and has now started wetting the bed.

## What else should I know about bed-wetting?

- Most children stop wetting the bed by 7 or 8 years old.

- Bed-wetting can last into the teen years and then stop.

# Your Child's Skin 10

Notes

_____

_____

_____

_____

_____

_____

_____

_____

_____

_____

_____

_____

_____

_____

# Chicken Pox

## What is it?

It's an illness with red spots, blisters, and scabs that show up all over the body. They cause a bad itch. Chicken pox can pass from person to person.

## What do I see?

- Fever
- Your child seems tired
- A clear blister on a red spot or bump that looks like a dewdrop on a rose petal
- New spots show up every day for 3–5 days

## What can I do at home?

- Give your child a bath with cool water. Add a cup of baking soda to the tub to help the itch.
- Give acetaminophen for fever, if your child is older than 2 years.
- Cut your child's fingernails.
- Try to keep your child from scratching the red spots.
- Use calamine lotion on red spots to help the itch.

- Never give aspirin to a child with chicken pox. Do not give aspirin for any reason to children younger than 21 years old.
- Put socks or cotton gloves on the hands of young children. This will protect the skin from scratching.
- Keep your child away from other people who have not had chicken pox.
- Keep your child indoors and away from the sun.

## When do I call the doctor or nurse?

- Itching cannot be stopped.
- There are sores in the eyes or private parts.
- Your child has any of these problems:
  - high fever
  - bad headache
  - vomiting
  - bad cough
  - stiff neck
  - seizure
  - forgets things
  - difficulty breathing
- Your child has pain when peeing.
- The spots look infected. They may be:
  - oozing pus
  - swollen
  - very red
  - very sore

- Your child will not drink, or he has less pee than before.
- Your child has a new fever **after** the first 2–3 days of illness.

## What else should I know about chicken pox?

- There is a shot to prevent chicken pox. It can be given to children at 1 year or older. Ask your doctor about this shot.
- It takes 10–21 days for a child to get chicken pox after being close to someone who has chicken pox.
- Most spots heal with no long-term marks. Scratching can cause marks that do not go away. They are called scars.
- Children can pass chicken pox to other people for about 7 days. This can happen even before red spots show up.
- When a child has chicken pox, you first see red spots, called pox marks. These turn into blisters, and then scabs.
- When all pox marks turn into scabs, your child can no longer give chicken pox to others. This is when your child can go back to school.

# Diaper Rash

## What is it?

Red, raw spots on a baby's bottom or thighs (the area covered by a diaper). Most babies get diaper rash. Dirty diapers cause most diaper rash.

## What do I see?

- Red, raw skin under the diaper
- Red spots can spread to thighs, belly, and back.

## What can I do at home?

- Change the diaper as soon as it gets wet.
- Feel the diaper every hour, even during the night. Change it if it is wet.
- Clean your baby's bottom at each diaper change. Use plain warm water.
- Keep the diaper off as long as you can. Keep it off at least 15 minutes at each diaper change.
- Dry your baby's bottom well. Put on Desitin or zinc oxide ointment with each diaper change.
- Do not use plastic pants. They keep the skin wet.
- Do not use baby wipes. They can cause a rash and may hurt your baby's skin.

- Use one of these mild soaps to wash cloth diapers:
  - Ivory Snow
  - Cheer Free for Sensitive Skin
  - Baby Soft
  - Dreft

## When do I call the doctor or nurse?

- The rash does not look better in 3 days.
- Red spots spread outside the diaper area.
- Red spots:
  - get bigger
  - are bright red
  - watery
  - turn into open sores
  - get infected
- Your baby seems sick.
- The rash gets very shiny.

## What else should I know about diaper rash?

- If your baby gets a diaper rash, try using another brand of diapers.
- Powders can make diaper rash worse. They should not be used.
- Pee and poop hurt the skin and make the rash worse. Keep your baby dry and clean all the time.
- Creams with zinc oxide protect baby's skin from pee and poop.

# Eczema

## What is it?

Eczema is dry, itchy skin. It often runs in families. It's usually worse in babies and children. It gets better as children get older.

## What do I see?

- Red, dry skin on cheeks, behind ears, on inside of elbows, and the back of knees.
- Skin feels like it has small bumps on it.
- Skin may ooze clear liquid and crust over.

## What can I do at home?

- Do not do things that dry the skin like giving long hot baths.
- Give your child short, cool baths. Keep them to 5 minutes or less. Soap dries the skin. Use very little of a mild soap such as Dove.
- Pat the skin dry after the bath. Don't rub the skin with a towel.
- Apply an unscented (no perfume) cream or lotion to the skin. Do this while the skin is moist after the bath. Put cream or lotion on the skin 3–4 times a day, so your child's skin feels soft.
- Use a mild soap when washing clothes.

- Avoid foods that make your child feel itchy.

- Do not touch or go near things that make the itch worse. Keep your child in soft cotton clothing. Don't put on wool or tight clothing such as spandex.

- Try to keep your child from scratching. Keep her fingernails short and hands clean.

- If your doctor orders a cream, use it as the doctor tells you.

- Ask your doctor if you can give Benadryl at night to stop the itch. Ask how much medicine to give.

## When do I call the doctor or nurse?

- The rash shows signs of infection such as redness, oozing pus, and feeling hot.

- Your child has a fever.

- Your child cannot sleep because of the itching.

- Your child looks or acts sick.

## What else should I know about eczema?

- Children can have other illnesses such as asthma and allergies along with eczema.

- The cream or lotion that you get from the doctor may hurt for a short time when you first put it on your child.

- If one kind of lotion makes the rash worse, do not use it.

- Eczema is a long-term skin problem. It is worse when the skin is dry. It may get better for a time, and then it may come back.

- Cold, dry weather makes eczema worse.

# Head Lice

## What is it?

Tiny bugs that live on the hair. They can also get into everything in the home.

## What do I see?

- Itchy head.
- Gray bugs that move fast.
- Many bugs may be on the back of the neck.
- Lice eggs (nits) may be stuck like glue on the hair close to the scalp. Eggs look like small, white specks.

## What can I do at home?

- Wash hair with a special hair shampoo or rinse made to kill lice. You can buy it at the drugstore. There are several you can use:
  - NIX hair rinse
  - RID shampoo
- Ask your doctor which one to use. Ask your doctor if it is OK to use the shampoo on babies younger than 1 year.
- These shampoos and hair rinses are poisons. Read the label. Use with care. Store them out of the reach of children.
- Use this shampoo on all the family.

- Use a fine-tooth comb to remove lice eggs from the hair.

- Use a good light to help see the lice eggs. Take off the white specks when the hair is damp. All the specks must be taken off the hair.

- Wash all combs, brushes, and hairbands with the same hair shampoo and hot water.

- Wash sheets, jackets, stuffed toys, and other things that touched your child's head. Use hot water.

- You can put stuffed toys in the dryer for 20 minutes to kill lice.

- You also need to vacuum mattresses, furniture, and rugs. Do this so the lice will not come back.

- Don't forget to clean the inside of your car.

## When do I call the doctor or nurse?

- Home care does not get rid of lice.
- Head lice keep coming back.
- Your child is younger than 1 year and has head lice.

## What else should I know about head lice?

- Head lice can happen even if your child is clean and well cared for.
- Tell the school if your child has head lice. Then other children in the class can be checked.
- Lice can live off the hair for a short time. Clean the house well, and keep children away from the lice.
- The lice shampoo may not kill all the lice eggs. You must take them off the hair. Use a fine-tooth comb.
- Check the heads of everyone living in the home every day for 7 days. Wash with special hair shampoo, if needed.
- Children can go back to school after washing with the special shampoo. All the specks must be out of the hair.
- You do not need to use bug spray on the furniture or house.
- Teach your children to not share head items with others. These include hats, combs, and headbands.

# Heat Rash

## What is it?

Tiny bumps that can be anywhere on a baby's body.

## What do I see?

- Tiny red or pink bumps on the neck, back, or shoulders.

## What can I do at home?

- Dress your baby lightly, and do not use creams or oils.
- Give your baby cool baths without soap, and let skin air dry.

## When do I call the doctor or nurse?

- The rash gets worse, or spots get bigger and watery.
- The rash is not better in 3 days, or your child has a fever.

## What else should I know about heat rash?

- Heat rash, also called prickly heat, comes mostly in hot weather.
- Children can get heat rash in cold weather if they are dressed too warmly. They can also get it if creams and oils are put on the skin.

# Hives

## What is it?

It's an allergic reaction to food, bug bites, or other things that cause red or pink spots on the skin.

## What do I see?

- Raised, red, or pink spots in different sizes called welts.
- Your child is very itchy.

## What can I do at home?

- Give your child cool baths.
- Put calamine lotion on hives for itch.
- Ask your doctor if you can give Benadryl for the itch. Ask how much medicine to give. Diphenhydramine is the same as Benadryl but costs less.
- Stay away from the thing that gave your child the hives. Try to think of what your child did or ate that is new.

## When do I call the doctor or nurse?

- Your child has a hard time breathing or swallowing. **Call 911.**
- Your child's tongue gets bigger. **Call 911.**
- Your child has belly (stomach) pain, fever, or joint pains.
- Hives do not go away in 1–2 days.

## What else should I know about hives?

- See Food Allergies, p. 108, for foods that can cause hives.
- You may never know what gave your child hives.

# Impetigo
# (Infected Sores)

## What is it?

An infection of the skin that is easy to spread

## What do I see?

* Red sores anywhere on the body
* Sores begin to ooze. Then they turn yellow or honey color and crusty.
* Sores can spread from one part of the body to another.

## What can I do at home?

* Soak the sores in warm soapy water for 15–20 minutes. Do this 2 to 3 times a day to take the crust off.
* Use a medicine soap such as Betadine. You can buy it at the drugstore. Pat the sores dry.
* Put a medicine ointment such as Polysporin on the sores. Put it on 2 to 3 times a day, after the crust is off. You can buy Polysporin at the drugstore.
* Cover sores with a clean bandage. Don't let your child touch or scratch the sores.
* Some impetigo needs medicine from a doctor. If the doctor orders medicine, be sure to give it for as long as your doctor tells you.

- Do these things to stop the spread of impetigo:
  - Wash your hands with soap after touching your child's sores or his clothes and towels.
  - Wash your child's hands very well. Cut your child's fingernails short.
  - Try to keep your child's fingers out of his nose.
  - Keep child's clothes, towels, and other things separate from others. Wash them with soap and very hot water.

## When do I call the doctor or nurse?

- You think your child has impetigo.
- The sores get bigger.
- The sores go to other places on your child's body.
- Your child looks or acts sick.
- Your child has swollen or sore joints. These include the elbows or knees.

## What else should I know about impetigo?

- Impetigo spreads easily from one person to another. This happens by touching sores or things that touched sores.
- Children can go to school if clothes cover the sores, and the sores have been treated for more than 2 days.
- Impetigo can make a child very sick. Take your child to the doctor right away if the sores spread or get bigger.
- Impetigo is very bad for new babies. Wash your hands very well before touching your baby. Do not let children with impetigo touch your baby or your baby's things.

# Poison Ivy or Poison Oak

## What is it?

A red, raised rash that comes after touching a poison ivy or poison oak plant. It may also come from touching something that has touched one of these plants.

## What do I see?

- Red, raised bumps
- Itchy rash
- Rash appears 12–48 hours after your child touches the plant

Poison ivy

## What can I do at home?

- Do these things if your child comes in contact with poison ivy:
  - Run lots of water over the skin right away.
  - Take your child's clothes off.
  - Bathe the skin with soap and water.
- Wash clothes and other things that came in contact with the plant with soap and very hot water. Wear rubber gloves when touching these things.
- Pets can carry poison ivy on their fur. Wash pets if you think they came in contact with poison ivy or poison oak.

- Scratching can spread the plant oil to other body areas. Wash well under your child's nails.

- Do these things if your child has an itchy rash:
  - Give her cool baths. Put Aveeno oatmeal bath or baking soda in the water to help the itch. You can buy this in a store.
  - Put calamine lotion on the rash.
  - You can make a paste at home for the rash. Mix 3 teaspoons of baking soda and 1 teaspoon of water. Put this on the rash.

- Do this for a rash that is oozing clear yellow fluid:
  - Mix 2 teaspoons of baking soda in 4 cups of water.
  - Cover the rash with a cloth soaked in the baking soda water. Do this for 10 minutes 4 times a day.

- Cut your child's fingernails short. Keep your child from scratching the rash.

- Wash your hands well. Don't touch your face.

- Ask your doctor if you can give Benadryl to stop the itch. Ask how much medicine to give. Diphenhydramine is the same as Benadryl but costs less.

## When do I call the doctor or nurse?

- Your child gets a fever or swelling of the face or eyes.
- Your child gets swelling in the groin, under the arms, or on the sides of the neck.
- Your child has very bad itching that won't let him sleep.
- Your child has redness or pus (thick white, yellow, or green liquid) oozing from the rash.

## What else should I know about poison ivy or poison oak?

- Show children what a poison ivy or poison oak plant looks like. Teach them not to touch it.
- The rash may last 2–3 weeks.

# Ringworm

## What is it?

Ringworm is an infection of the skin, scalp, and feet caused by a fungus. Ringworm has nothing to do with worms.

## What do I see?

- Round pink patch
- Clearing of the center as the patch grows
- Raised, rough, scaly border
- ½ to 1 inch in size
- Can get bigger if not treated
- May be itchy

## What can I do at home?

- Use an antifungal cream at least 2 times a day. This can be bought at the drugstore. Ask the pharmacist at the drugstore for an antifungal cream.
- Apply the cream to the whole rash and at least 1 inch around the rash.
- Apply the cream to the area of the rash for at least 7 days after the rash is gone.
- It may take up to 4 weeks to clear the rash.

## When do I call the doctor or nurse?

- Pus is draining from the rash.
- More than 3 spots are present.
- Ringworm continues to spread after 1 week of treatment.
- Ringworm has not cleared up in 4 weeks.
- Your child has ringworm on the scalp.

## What else should I know about ringworm?

- Ringworm of the skin may pass from child to child if there is direct skin-to-skin contact. After 48 hours of treatment you cannot pass ringworm to another person.
- Ringworm on the skin should be covered. Scalp ringworm does not have to be covered.
- If ringworm is covered, children do not have to miss school.
- Do not permit sharing of cloths, hats, combs, brushes, or other personal items.
- Frequent handwashing will help stop the spread of ringworm.
- Cut your child's fingernails short to stop the spread of ringworm.
- Dogs and cats can get ringworm. They can pass ringworm to people.

# Scabies

## What is it?

Itchy skin rash that is caused by tiny bugs

## What do I see?

- Tiny pink bumps spread in a line on the body.
- Lots of itching that is worse at night.
- Rash is often seen on fingers, wrists, armpits, waist, and private parts. It can be anywhere on the body.
- Babies may have rash on soles of their feet and palms of their hands.
- You will not be able to see the bugs because they are so small.

## What can I do at home?

- Put skin medicine your doctor orders all over the body.
- Your doctor may have the family use the skin medicine also.
- Wash all clothes, sheets, and towels in hot water.
- Ask your doctor if you can give Benadryl to stop the itch. Diphenhydramine is the same as Benadryl but costs less.

## When do I call the doctor or nurse?

- You think your child has scabies.

- You will need a prescription for the skin medicine.

## What else should I know about scabies?

- Itchy rash may last for 3–4 weeks after you use the medicine.

- The tiny bugs pass from one person to another by being close. They also can move from one part of the body to another part.

- The bugs cannot be seen with the eye.

- Scabies can happen to anyone. It is not a sign of being dirty or not bathing.

# Sunburn

## What is it?

Burn on the skin caused by the sun.

## What do I see?

- Skin turns red or pink with a 1st degree burn.
- Skin has blisters with a 2nd degree burn.
- Skin can be puffy and sore.

## What can I do at home?

- Give your child cool baths.
- Put a cool wet cloth or towel on the sunburn.
- Give acetaminophen for pain, if your child is older than 2 years.
- Aloe vera gel helps with the pain.
- Do not use butter, ointments, or any other skin lotion such as benzocaine on the sunburn.
- Give your child more water or liquids to drink.
- Do not use soap on your child's skin for a few days.
- Dress your child with cool, soft clothing.
- Do not break open blisters. Blisters can get infected if you pop them. If a blister breaks, wash it with mild soap and water. Let it air dry.

## When do I call the doctor or nurse?

- Your child has a fever.
- The light is hard on your child's eyes.
- Your child is in a lot of pain.
- Your child has blisters on the skin.

## What can I do to prevent sunburn?

- Keep babies younger than 6 months in the shade. Protect your baby with a hat, long sleeves, and pants.
- Do not use sunscreen on babies younger than 6 months.
- Never put babies in the direct sun.
- For children older than 6 months, use a sunscreen with a sun factor (SPF) of 30 or higher. Do this even on cloudy days. Put sunscreen on at least 30 minutes before going out. Read the label and do what it says. Put more sunscreen on every 2-3 hours while outside.

- Be sure to put sunscreen on the child's ears. Don't forget the top of your child's feet.
- Children with thin hair should have sunscreen put on their head when not wearing a hat.
- Put sunscreen on again after swimming or sweating.
- Do not put sunscreen near lips, mouth, or on hands. This prevents young children from eating sunscreen lotion. Wash off sunscreen if it gets on your baby's hands or near the mouth.

- Your child can get sunburn in the eyes. Your child should wear sunglasses and a hat that shades the face. The sunglasses should give 100% UV protection.

## What else should I know about sunburn?

- Sunburn is bad for the skin. It can cause cancer.

- Children with dark skin, including African American children, can get sunburn. They need to use sunscreen.

- Some children can get a bad sunburn in just 15 minutes. Make sure your child always uses sunscreen when outside.

- Your child can get a sunburn while in a car. Use window shades to keep the sun off your child.

- Your child can get a sunburn even on a cloudy day. Clouds do not protect your child from sunburn. Put sunscreen and a hat on your child whenever he goes outside.

- Your child can get a sunburn through light or thin clothing. Put sunscreen on under your child's t-shirt and pants.

- Your child can get sunburn through wet clothes.

- Water makes the sun stronger. Your child can get a bad sunburn while playing in the water. Put sunscreen on your child often. Do not let your child play in the water in the sun.

- Teach your child to always put on sunscreen when going outside.

# What to Do When Your Child Gets Hurt 11

## Notes

_____

_____

_____

_____

_____

_____

_____

_____

_____

_____

_____

_____

_____

_____

_____

# Animal or Human Bites

## What is it?
A bite from a person or an animal.
Animals include dogs, cats, rats, or others.

## What do I see?
- The skin may have teeth marks on it.
- The skin may be broken. There may be some bleeding.
- The area may be warm and red. Pus may ooze from it.

## What can I do at home?
- If there is bleeding, press on the area. Use a clean cloth.
- Wash the skin with soap and warm water.
- Cover broken skin with a Band-Aid or bandage.
- Find out if the animal that bit your child had rabies shots.

## When do I call the doctor or nurse?
- The bite broke your child's skin.
- The bite is from a wild animal.
- The bite is from a pet that may not have had its shots.
- The animal is acting strangely.
- The animal has foam coming out of the mouth.
- Your child has signs of infection, such as fever, redness, pain, or swelling.

## What else should I know about animal bites?

- All pets should have rabies shots.
- Teach your child not to touch animals he does not know.
- Teach your child to stay away from animals that are eating.
- Never leave a young child alone with a dog or other animal.
- Do not allow children to tease or hurt animals.

# Bleeding

## What is it?

Fast bleeding or bleeding that does not stop easily.

## What do I see?

- Bright red blood is coming out of a break in the skin.
- Your child may seem weak.
- Your child may not know where he or she is.
- Your child may go into a deep sleep (faint or pass out).

## What can I do at home?

- Have your child lie down.
- Place the bleeding part higher than the heart.

- Keep your child warm.
- Take out anything from the cut or sore that is easy to wipe away. Do not try to pull out things that are deep or hard to get out.

- Do not try to cut anything out.
- Put a clean cloth over the bleeding area. Press hard.
- If cloth gets too bloody, place another cloth on top of that one. Do not take the first cloth off the area.
- Do not stop pressing. Do not press so hard that it hurts.
- If bone or something else is sticking out of the cut, put pressure around the cut. Do not press right on top of it.

## When do I call the doctor or nurse?

- **Call 911** if blood is pouring out, and you can't stop it.
- A bone or something else is sticking out of the cut.
- You cannot stop the bleeding by pressing on the area.

## What else should I know about bleeding?

- Your child can lose too much blood from bleeding. This is called shock.
  **Call 911 if your child shows any signs of shock.**
- **Signs of shock:**
  - Pupils get big (black dots in the center of the eyes).
  - Skin feels cool and wet.
  - Pulse (heartbeat) is fast and weak.
  - Breathing is fast.
  - Your child is sick to the stomach (nausea).
  - Your child throws up (vomits).

- Your child wants to drink (**do not give your child anything to drink**).
- Your child does not know where he is (confused).
- Your child is weak.
- Your child goes into a deep sleep and cannot be woken up.

# Broken Bone

## What is it?

A crack or break in a bone.
It comes from a fall or accident.

## What do I see?

- Your child is in a lot of pain.

- The area around the bone swells up.

- Your child may refuse to use the leg or arm.

- The bone under the skin may look bent.

- You may see the bone if the skin is broken.

- You may hear the bone crack at the time of the fall.

## What can I do at home?

- Put a splint on an arm or leg that is broken. A splint is anything you can tie to a body part to stop it from moving. A rolled-up newspaper, magazine, or stick may be used as a splint.

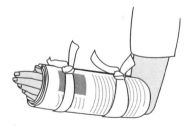

- Never tie the body to the splint so tight that blood can't move to the area.

- If you think a leg bone is broken, do not let your child walk on it.

- Ice helps pain and swelling. Do not put ice right on the skin. Wrap it in a towel. Leave it on for 5 minutes or less each time.

- Do not give your child anything to eat or drink until you see the doctor.

- **Do not wait to take your child to your doctor or clinic.** A broken bone should be checked right away.

## When do I call the doctor or nurse?

- You think your child has a broken bone.

## What can I do to prevent broken bones?

- Never leave a young child alone on a high place even for a few seconds. This includes sofas, changing tables, or shopping carts. Your child can have a bad fall.

- Keep crib rails up to your baby's chin at all times.

- Do not use a baby walker. Your baby can tip over or crash through a safety gate.

- Put safety locks on your windows. Your child can open a window and fall out.

## What should I know about sprains?

- Your doctor may tell you that your child has a sprain, and not a broken bone. This is not as bad as a broken bone. A sprain can give your child a lot of pain.

- Ice helps pain and swelling. Wrap ice in a cloth, and put it on the sprain. Leave it on for 5 minutes or less each time.

- Rest the joint on a pillow higher than the body. Keep your child from using the joint.

- Give ibuprofen for pain, if your child is older than 2 years.

- Your doctor may tell you to use a heating pad or a warm damp towel on the sprain after the first 24 hours.

- Call your doctor or nurse if the sprain is not better in 3–4 days.

# Bruises

## What is it?

Dark marks on the skin. Bleeding under the skin causes them. Bruises happen when your child falls or gets hurt. It takes about 2 weeks for a bruise to go away. Bruises can be a sign of abuse.

## What do I see?

- The skin has a black, brown, blue, purple, green, or yellow mark on it.
- The skin may turn red at first.
- You may see or feel a bump.

## What can I do at home?

- Most bruises do not need any care.
- You can put ice on large bruises. Wrap the ice in a cloth. Leave it on for 5 minutes or less each time.
- After 24–48 hours, heat may help. Use a heating pad on low or a warm damp cloth.

## When do I call the doctor or nurse?

- Your child gets bruises without falling or getting hurt.
- You think a bone may be broken.
- Your child has bruises in unusual places such as the ear or stomach.

# Bug Bites

## What is it?

A painful or itchy bite from a bug. The bite may be from a bee, tick, flea, ant, fly, spider, wasp, mosquito, or other insect.

## What do I see?

* Area gets bigger (swells)
* Redness
* Your child's whole body can get red, and swell.
* Your child may find it hard to breathe.

## What can I do at home?

* There may be a stinger left in the skin. Do not pull out a stinger with tweezers.
  * Take out a stinger by scraping it gently with your fingernail.
  * Try not to break the stinger.
  * You can also scrape off the stinger with the edge of a credit card.
* Wrap ice in a cloth. Put it on the bite for 5 minutes or less each time.
* Mix baking soda and water into a paste. Put it on the bite if your child has pain.
* Put calamine lotion on the bite to stop the itch.

161

- Cut your child's fingernails. Keep them short, so they won't hurt if your child scratches.

## When do I call the doctor or nurse?

- **Call 911** if your child finds it hard to breath or her face swells. This is an emergency.
- Your child gets a rash all over the body. He gets itchy and swollen after the bite. This may be an allergic reaction.
- There are signs of infection such as swelling, yellow pus oozing out of the bite, or fever. This can happen later.
- Your child is in a lot of pain. She looks and acts sick.
- Your child is younger than 3 months old and gets a bug bite.

## What else should I know about bug bites?

- Have your child wear long-sleeve shirts and pants. This will keep your child from getting bug bites.
- Your child should not wear perfume or other sweet-smelling lotions outside.
- Put insect spray on your child. Read the label well and do what it says. Keep insect spray away from the face.
- Teach your child to stay away from beehives and other places where bugs are.
- Find out where the bugs are. Have your child stay away from dogs or cats with fleas or ticks and friends' houses that have bugs.
- Do not go outdoors around sunset.

# Bump on the Head

## What is it?

Your child gets hit on the head. Your child falls and hits the head.

## What do I see?

- Your child may have a big lump on the head.
- Your child may have a cut on the head with some bleeding.
- Your child may have a seizure (convulsion).
- Your child may faint or pass out.
- Your child may throw up (vomit).
- Your child may be confused.

## What can I do at home?

- If your child has bleeding, hold a towel firmly on the area for 10–15 minutes.
- Put an ice pack on the bump. You can wrap some ice in a cloth.
- Your child may have had only a light bump to the head. He went back to playing after a short cry. In this case, you can take care of your child at home. Be sure to watch for anything not normal. Call your doctor right away if you have any questions.

- Wake your child up every 2 hours for the first 24 hours. Look for changes in your child's eyes. Check for weakness in one side of the body. Watch for any vomiting. Ask your child some things that he should know.

## When do I call the doctor or nurse?

- Your child fainted or passed out after the fall. It may be for only a moment.
- You can't stop the bleeding from a cut on the head.
- Your child cries for more than 10 minutes. He will not stop.
- Your child has a seizure (convulsion).
- Your child gets sleepy. She is hard to wake up.
- Your child does not know things as well as before.
- Your child does not talk or walk as well as before.
- Your child's eyes do not look the same. The eyes may be crossed or the pupils (black dots in the center of the eyes) are not the same size.
- Blood or water is coming out of your child's ears or nose.
- Your child has forceful vomiting or vomits more than once.
- Your child seems confused.

## What can I do to prevent head injuries?

- Always put a helmet on your child for certain sports. These include bike riding, rollerblading, skateboarding, and scootering. The helmet should cover the top of your child's forehead.

- Put your child in the back seat of the car. This is the safest place for your child. Always put your child in a car seat or seat belt when driving in the car.

- If you have a passenger air bag, **never** put your child in the front seat. Car makers recommend rear seating for all children 12 years and younger.

- Use a car seat until a child is 8 years old, unless they are 4 feet and 9 inches tall or taller.

- The car seat you use depends on your child's age and weight. Read the papers that come with the car seat to make sure it is right for your child.

  - Babies should ride in a rear-facing car seat. Keep babies facing the back of the car until they are over 2 years old and are bigger than the height and weight for their car seat.

  - Once your child grows out of the rear-facing seat and is over 2 years old, place him in a toddler car seat that faces the front of the car.

  - There are state laws about when to put a child in a booster seat. Check with your doctor or nurse.

- Never leave your child alone in a high place where she can fall.

- Keep crib rails up to your baby's chin at all times.

- Place a gate to keep your child away from steps.

- Lock all doors that lead to steps.

- Never shake or hit your baby. Your baby's brain is very soft. A baby can be badly hurt and die from shaking.

# Burns

## What is it?

An injury to the skin. Heat, hot liquids, steam, gas, electric shock, or chemicals may cause it.

There are 3 kinds of burns:

- 1st degree — The outer layer of skin is burned.
- 2nd degree — The deeper skin is burned.
- 3rd degree — These are very deep burns.

## What do I see?

- The skin may be red, hot to the touch, and painful.
- The skin may be white, brown, or black instead of red.
- The skin may be puffy.
- There may be blisters on the skin.

## What can I do at home?

- You can use water to put out fires, except grease fires.
- Use baking soda or a fire extinguisher for a grease fire.
- If your child's clothes are on fire, your child will be scared and run. You should:
  - Catch your child quickly. Roll your child on the ground to put out the fire.
  - Cover your child with a blanket, coat, or rug to put out the fire.

- Run cold water on the burned skin right away. This stops the skin from burning more. It also helps the pain.
- Do not put ice on the skin.
- Take off burned clothing unless it is stuck to the skin.
- If the skin is oozing, cover it with a clean cloth.
- If the skin is dry, cover the burn with a cool, wet, clean cloth.

- Do not put butter, grease, or powder on the burn.
- Give acetaminophen for pain, if your child is older than 2 years.
- Do not break open blisters. If blisters break, wash them with soap and water. Cover them with a clean cloth.

## When do I call the doctor or nurse?

- The burn is larger than the size of your child's hand.
- There are blisters on the skin.
- The burn is on the face, hands, feet, private parts, or a moving joint, such as the knee.
- You think the burn is bad.
- The burned skin is white, brown, or black.
- There are signs of infection, such as swelling, pus, or fever.
- The burn is not better in 3 days.

## What can I do to prevent burns?

- Have smoke detectors in each bedroom and in the hallway. Put in new batteries every 6 months.

# Burns

- Have a fire extinguisher. Know how to use it.
- Teach children to stop, drop to the ground, and roll if their clothes catch on fire.
- Set your water heater at 120 degrees F. This will avoid burns from very hot water coming out of the faucet.
- Always test the bath water with your elbow. Make sure it is OK for your child.
- Keep children away from the stove, irons, and curling irons. Turn off and uplug these things when you are not using them.
- Keep matches, lighters, and other things that burn away from children.
- Teach children not to play with matches or other things that can cause a fire.
- Teach children what to do in case of fire.
- Children like to reach up and grab things. Turn pot handles away from your child's reach.
- Never hold your child while drinking a hot liquid such as coffee. Never hold your child while cooking by a hot stove.
- Never heat your child's bottle or food in a microwave oven. Some parts may get so hot they can burn your child.

# CPR
## (Cardiopulmonary Resuscitation)

## What is it?

CPR is what you should do when a baby or child stops breathing and the heart stops beating. A child's heart and breathing can stop from things, such as drowning, electrical shock, and choking. CPR gets air to the child and keeps the blood moving in the body. Many people have saved their child's life by doing CPR.

To learn how to do CPR, mouth-to-mouth breathing, or help a child who is choking, take a class called Basic Life Support. The American Red Cross, the American Heart Association, or your local hospital gives these classes. Call one of these places to find out how to take a class.

This book tells you what to do in an emergency. To do it right, you should take a class. In class you will be able to practice on a doll.

**Until you take a class in CPR, give chest presses only. Do not give breaths.**

## What do I see?

- The child's skin may be very pale or blue.
- The chest is not moving up and down.
- The child does not move. It looks like the child is in a deep sleep.

**169**

# CPR (Cardiopulmonary Resuscitation)

## What can I do for a baby (younger than 1 year)?

1. Try to wake your baby up. If your baby does not wake up, yell for help. Tell someone to **call 911**.

2. Lay your baby on something hard such as the floor or a table. Put the baby on his or her back.

3. Use one hand on the baby's forehead. Tilt the head back.

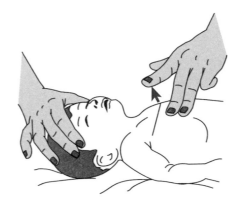

4. With your other hand place 2 or 3 fingers, 1-finger width below the middle of a pretend line drawn between the baby's nipples.

5. Press the baby's chest down 1½ inches.

6. Do this fast for 30 times. Count each press as you do a press.

7. Tilt the baby's head back. Do this by lifting the chin with one hand and pushing the forehead back with the other hand. Do not close your baby's mouth.

8. If baby is not breathing, start mouth-to-mouth breathing. Open your mouth and take a breath. Cover your baby's nose and mouth with your mouth. Make a tight seal.

9. Keep the chin lifted. The head tilted back. The mouth open.

10. Give 2 slow breaths into the baby. The breaths should be 1 second long. Take a breath yourself between breaths into the baby. Look at the baby's chest to see if it goes up and down. Keep the baby's head tilted back with the mouth open.

11. If you can't get the baby's chest to go up and down the first time you blow into the baby's nose and mouth, try again. If the chest does not move a second time, follow the things to do on pages 70-73 for a choking baby.

12. Give 30 fast presses to the chest. Press the baby's chest down 1½ inches. Follow this with 2 breaths into the baby. Give 30 chest presses again. Give the baby 100 chest presses and at least 6 breaths per minute. Count out loud to help you keep this rate.

13. After giving CPR for 2 minutes, check if the baby is breathing by putting your ear next to his mouth.

171

14. Do not stop CPR until your baby is OK, or someone else takes over. If you're alone, after 5 sets of 2 breaths and 30 pushes, call **911**, then keep doing CPR.

## What can I do for a child (older than 1 year and less than 8 years old)?

1. Try to wake the child up. If the child does not wake up, yell for help. Tell someone to **call 911.**

2. Lay the child on his back on something hard such as the floor.

3. Place the heel of one hand on the lower half of the breastbone. Press the child's chest down 1 to 1½ inches. You should be on your knees at the side of the child. Give 30 presses.

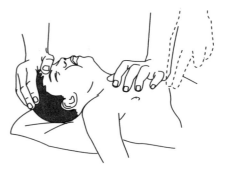

4. If the child is not breathing, begin mouth-to-mouth breathing. Tilt the child's head back by lifting the chin with one hand and pushing forehead back with the other hand. Do not close the mouth.

5. Hold the child's nose closed with your thumb and finger. Still hold the head back. Open your mouth wide and take a deep breath. Cover the child's mouth with your mouth. Make a tight seal over the child's mouth. Give 2 slow breaths into the child. The breaths should be 1 second long. Take a breath yourself between breaths into the child.

6. Look at the child's chest to see if it goes up and down. Keep your child's head tilted back with his mouth open.

7. If you can't get your child's chest to go up and down the first time you blow into her mouth, try again. If the chest does not move a second time, follow the things to do on pages 70-73 for a choking child.

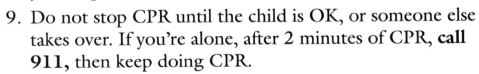

8. Give 30 presses. Give 2 breaths. Give at least 6 breaths each minute and 100 presses each minute. Count out loud to help you keep this rate.

9. Do not stop CPR until the child is OK, or someone else takes over. If you're alone, after 2 minutes of CPR, **call 911,** then keep doing CPR.

# CPR (Cardiopulmonary Resuscitation)

## What can I do for adults (and children more than 8 years old)?

The procedure is the same as for young children with the following differences:

1. Use 2-handed compressions 2 inches deep at the child's central region of the chest

2. Same ratio: 30 compressions to 2 breathes. After 2 minutes call 911 and continue CPR

## When should I call the doctor?

- Take your child to the emergency room right away if your child has been given CPR.

- You are not sure if your child needs to be seen in an emergency room.

- You are not sure that your child is OK.

## What else should I know about CPR?

- The American Heart Association, the American Red Cross, and hospitals teach **CPR**. You should take a class to be ready for an emergency.

- Start CPR as soon as your child is not breathing. Do CPR for 2 minutes, and then **call 911** if no one comes to help.

# Cuts and Scrapes

## What is it?

A break or injury to the skin.

## What do I see?

- The skin is red, open, and bleeding.
- There may be some swelling.

## What can I do at home?

- Stop the bleeding by pressing on the cut with a clean cloth for 10 minutes.

- Wash the cut well with soap and water. Be sure to wash away any dirt.

- Keep the cut clean. You can put a medicine ointment such as Polysporin on the cut. You can buy Polysporin at the drugstore. Cover the cut with a Band-Aid.

- Put a fresh Band-Aid on every day. Change it whenever it gets dirty.

- Take the Band-Aid off at least once a day. If the Band-Aid sticks, soak it off with warm water.

- Check the cut for signs of infection, such as redness, swelling, and pus oozing out.

## When do I call the doctor or nurse?

- The bleeding does not stop after 10 minutes of pressing.
- The cut is deep or the edges of the skin do not stay together.
- The cut happened outside in the dirt or from a nail or other dirty metal.
- There are red lines on the skin near the cut.
- There is swelling around the cut, and pus is oozing out of the cut.
- You see something in the cut that you cannot get out.

## What else should I know about cuts and scrapes?

- Most cuts and scrapes heal well with care at home.
- If there is a lot of bleeding, turn to page 154 for what to do.

# Drowning

## What is it?
A child is under water and can't breathe.

## What do I see?
- The child's face is under water.
- The child may cry and cough when pulled out of the water.
- The child may be limp and not breathing when pulled out.

## What can I do at home?
- Pull the child out of the water.
- Yell for help. Have someone **call 911.**
- Lay the child on her back.
- Check to see if the child is breathing (see page 170).
- **Do CPR** if child is not breathing (see page 170).

## When do I call the doctor or nurse?
- Your child was under water for more than a few seconds.

## What can I do to prevent drowning?
- A young child can drown in a very small amount of water, such as a pail of water. Do not leave water in pails.
- Empty baby pools when not in use.

# Drowning

- A small child can also drown in the toilet. Put a latch on the toilet lid. Lock the bathroom door, or use a safety gate to keep your baby out of the bathroom.

- Never leave your child alone near water. Don't risk it even for a few seconds.

- Do not leave your child alone in the tub. Don't risk it even for a few seconds.

- Put fences around pools, spas, ponds, and other bodies of water.

- Teach your child how to swim at around 4 years old. **Always stay with your child.** A child who knows how to swim can still drown.

- Teach your child not to go near water alone.

- Teach your child to always swim with an adult.

# Poisoning

## What is it?

Your child eats or breathes something that makes him sick. Your child can get poisoned from many things. These include cleaning products, vitamins, drugs, medicines, alcohol, paint, and plants. Poisoning is very serious. Your child can die.

## What do I see?

- You find your child with a bottle or container of something that is poison. The bottle may be open or empty.
- Your child has burns on the lips or in the mouth.
- Your child feels like throwing up.
- Your child throws up for no reason.
- Your child is hard to wake up.
- Your child has a hard time breathing.
- Your child has stomach pain.
- Your child has a fit (seizure or convulsion).

# Poisoning

## What can I do at home?

- If you think your child has swallowed a poison, stay calm.

- If your child is having trouble breathing or you can't wake up your child, call **911 right away**.

- If the child is awake, **call the poison control center right away**. The number that can be used anywhere in the U.S.A. is 1-800-222-1222. Write this number down, and keep it next to the phone so you can find it when you need it. Save this number in your phone. If you don't have this number, call **911**.

- Try to tell the poison control center:
  - The child's age and weight
  - The name of the medicine or poison that was taken, if known
  - The amount that was taken, if known
  - The time the poison was taken
  - Your name and phone number

- Do what the poison control center tells you to do.

- **Do not** give syrup of ipecac. **Do not** make your child vomit unless poison control tells you it is OK or your doctor told you to do so.

- **Do not** give your child lots of water to drink unless the poison control center tells you to do so.

# Poisoning

## What can I do to prevent poisoning?

- Buy medicines with childproof caps.

- Store medicines and vitamins out of your child's reach.

- If you have people over to your house, ask if they have any medicines. Put their medicines out of your child's reach.

- Never tell children that medicine is candy.

- Read the label well before giving your child medicine. Many mistakes happen at night. Turn the light on, and take a good look at the label on the bottle.

- Don't give your child someone else's medicine.

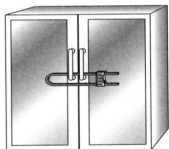

- Store all cleaning products and other poisons in locked cabinets. Your child could eat them.

- Do not keep soap, cleaning products, or anything else under the kitchen or bathroom sink.

- Always keep things in the bottles they came in. Do not put poisons in food jars or bottles.

- Don't let your child peel off old paint and eat it. Your child can get lead poisoning.

- Never mix cleaning products together, such as bleach and ammonia. It can give off a poison gas that can make you or someone else very sick.

- Do not take medicine in front of your child. They may want to do the same thing and take the medicine too.

## What else should I know about poisoning?

- Teach your babysitter what to do in case of poisoning.
- Teach your child how to **call 911.**
- Poisoning can occur if your child eats certain plants around the house or outside. Do not let your child near plants unless you are sure they are not poison. Ask your doctor or nurse if you are not sure.
- Turn on a fan and open the windows when using harsh cleaning products that smell or have fumes.
- Wear gloves, long pants, long sleeves, socks, and shoes when spraying for bugs, pests, or using other chemicals. Keep your child away.
- Do not burn fuels or charcoal or use gas engines in small spaces such as a garage, tent, or poorly aired rooms.

# Word List

## A

- **airway**—Breathing tube going from the back of the throat to the lungs.
- **allergy**—Getting sick (itching, sneezing, hives, hard breathing, or even fainting) from something such as medicine, food, plant, dust, or other things.
- **antibiotic**—A medicine ordered by the doctor to kill germs that cause infection.
- **asthma**—An illness that causes tightness of the airway or breathing tube brought on by a cold, or coming in contact with smoke, dust, pets, or other things the child is allergic to.
- **axilla**—The underarm or armpit.

## B

- **bacteria**—Germs that can make you sick.
- **belly button**—The place in the middle of the belly where the cord was attached when you were born.
- **blister**—A raised area of skin filled with a water-like liquid.
- **blurred**—Can't see clearly.
- **bowel movement (BM)**—The way we pass solid material (waste) from the body. Also called stool or poop.
- **breathing**—Taking air into and letting it out of the lungs.
- **bulging out**—Swelling or popping out.

# Word List

## C

- **cavity**—A hole in a tooth caused by decay.
- **chills**—Feeling cold and shaking.
- **colic**—Crying that lasts 3–4 hours for 3–4 days.
- **coma**—A deep sleep-like state caused by sickness or injury.
- **convulsion**—Sudden movements of a person or part of a person's body that the person cannot control. Also called a seizure.
- **coughing spasm**—Cough that cannot be stopped for a long time.
- **crusty**—Dried old skin or liquid on the body.

## D

- **dehydration**—The loss of too much liquid from the body.
- **dentist**—Doctor for the teeth.
- **diphenhydramine**—Generic word for Benadryl.
- **disease**—Sickness or illness.
- **dizzy**—Feels like the room is spinning or turning around.
- **drooling**—Liquid coming out of the mouth.
- **drugstore**—A store where you can buy medicine.

## E

- **eardrum**—A thin skin deep in the ear that moves with sound and helps you hear.
- **ear tubes**—Tiny plastic tubes put in the eardrum by the doctor to drain liquid out of the ears.
- **elevate**—To lift up, put high.
- **eyelid**—Skin that covers the eye.
- **eczema**—skin problem that causes dry, red, itchy skin.

# Word List

## F

- **faint**—To feel weak and fall to the floor.
- **fever**—The body is hotter than normal.
- **flare**—To open wider.
- **floss**—To clean between the teeth.
- **fluoride**—Something in water that makes teeth strong.

## G

- **germs**—Something you cannot see that can make you sick.
- **groin**—The front part of the body between the legs where the legs join the body.

## H

- **humidifier**—A machine that puts a mist of water into the air.

## I

- **immunizations**—Shots given at certain times to protect against certain diseases. Also called vaccinations.
- **injury**—To get hurt.
- **irritated**—A sore area of the body.

## L

- **label**—Paper on a medicine bottle that tells you how to give the medicine. It also tells you what is in it, and other things about the medicine. Always read the label before giving medicine.
- **lukewarm water**—Water that is not hot and not cold. It feels the same temperature as the body.

## M

- **medicine**—Something you take into or put on the body to make you better.

- **mucus**—A thick liquid made by the body that protects the nose, throat, and other parts of the body. Mucus can flow out of the body during sickness.

## N

- **navel**—The belly button. The place in the middle of the belly where the cord was attached when your baby was born.
- **nostril**—The nose opening.

## O

- **ointment**—A medicine you put on the skin or in the eyes.
- **oozing**—Liquid coming out slowly.
- **oral**—Refers to the mouth.
- **over-the-counter**—Medicines you can buy without an order (prescription) from a doctor.

## P

- **pacifier**—A nipple for your baby to suck on that calms her.
- **pee**—Urine. Liquid waste from the body.
- **pharmacist**—A person who gives you the medicine your doctor orders. The pharmacist can help you with over-the-counter medicine or other health supplies.
- **pimple**—A small red or white bump on the skin.
- **poison**—Something that makes you very sick if taken into the body.
- **prescription**—An order from the doctor for medicine.
- **pulse**—Blood moving through the body with the heartbeat.
- **pupil**—The black dot in the middle of the eye.
- **pus**—A thick liquid that comes out of the body when there is infection. The liquid is usually yellow or green and can smell bad.

## R

- **rash**—Red spots on the skin.
- **rectal**—Refers to the rectum.
- **rectum**—Where BMs (bowel movements) come out.
- **ringworm**—An infection of the skin, scalp, or feet caused by a fungus, not a worm.
- **rot**—To go bad, spoil, or decay.
- **rubbing alcohol**—Not for drinking. Clear liquid used to clean thermometers and other things.

## S

- **scab**—Hard brown crust on the skin from the healing of a sore, pimple, or cut.
- **secondhand smoke**—Breathing air that has smoke from cigarettes.
- **seizure**—Sudden movements of a person's body (all or part) that the person cannot control. Also called a convulsion.
- **shiver**—To shake from cold or fever.
- **shampoo**—Soap for the hair.
- **shock**—A very bad condition with weakness or unconsciousness, cold sweat, and weak pulse.
- **shots**—Another word for immunizations. They are given at certain times to protect against diseases.
- **smoke detector**—A device that makes a loud sound from fire or smoke.
- **spasm**—A muscle contraction you cannot control.
- **stomach**—The place in the body where food goes. Used to mean the entire belly area.
- **suction bulb**—A thing used to suck mucus from the nose.

- **sunscreen**—Lotion put on the skin to prevent sunburn.
- **swallow**—To pass food from the mouth to the stomach.
- **swollen**—An area that gets bigger.

## T

- **temperature**—The degree of heat of a person's body.
- **thermometer**—A thing that is used to check the heat of the body.
- **tooth decay**—The rotting of teeth.

## U

- **unconscious**—Not being able to wake someone up.
- **urine**—Pee. Liquid waste from the body.
- **UV protection**—The thing in sunscreen that helps protect the skin from the sun.

## V

- **vaccinations**—Shots that are given at certain times and ages to stop people from getting bad illnesses. Also called immunizations.
- **viral**—Refers to virus.
- **virus**—Something too small to see that can pass from one person to another and make you sick.

## W

- **wind pipe**—The tube that goes from the back of the throat to the lungs.
- **wool**—A type of clothing material that is very warm.

# What's in This Book From A to Z

# What's in This Book From A to Z

# What's in This Book From A to Z

# What's in This Book From A to Z

# What's in This Book From A to Z

# What's in This Book From A to Z

# What's in This Book From A to Z

# People We Want to Thank

We thank the following people for their h/ with this book:

Albert Barnett, MD
Corby Bashaw
Gloria J. Bateman
Linda Bednar
Stephanie Renee Booth, MD
Margaret Brady, PhD, RN, CPNP
Ben A. Carlsen, Ed.D.
Lisa Deer
Robin King-Dodge
Dinesh Ghiya, MD
Diane Hebert, MPH
Marian Henry, RRT, MPH, CHES
Nancy Izuno
Laura Johnson
Nai Kang, MPH, CHES
Gary F. Krieger, MD
Judith Whitney Leonard, MSN, RN, CPNP
Rita London
Victor London
Patricia Lovera
Nancy McDade

Dora L. Millan
Dana Ma, MPH, CHES
Carol Mews, MPH
Thomas Mayer, MD
Ruby Ya-Morones, MD, MPH
Chaw Naughton
Michl O'Neal
Greg Perez, BS
Dores Ramos, RDH, BS
Php Rapa
Gy Richwald, MD, MPH
Adrey Riffenburgh, MA
Steven Rosenberg, MD, MPH
Nancy Rushton, BSN, RN
Duane Saikami, Pharm.D.
Alma Sanchez
Suzanne Snyder
Carole Talan, Ed.D.
Robert Vouga, MA, Ed.D.
Elaine Weiner, MPH, RN
Jacqueline Zazueta

# Oth Books in the Series

**What To Do
For Your Teen's Health**

The teen years are hard on parents and teens.
There are many things you can do to help your
teen. At last, an easy to read, easy to use book
written by two nurses. This book tells you:

- About the body changes that
  happen to teens.
- How to get ready for the teen years.
- How to talk with your teen.
- What you can do to feel closer to your teen.
- How to help your teen do well in school.
- All about dating and sex.
  How to keep your teen safe.
  The signs of trouble and
  where to go for help.

ISBN 978-0-9720148-9-2
$12.95

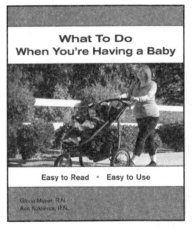

**What To Do
When You're Having a Baby**

There are many things a woman can do to have
a healthy baby. Here's an easy to read, easy to
use book written by two nurses that tells you:

- How to get ready for pregnancy.
- About the health care you need
  during pregnancy.
- Things you should not do
  when you are pregnant.
- How to take care of yourself
  so you have a healthy baby.
- Body changes you have each month.
- Simple things you can do to feel better.
- Warning signs of problems and
  what to do about them.
- All about labor and delivery.
- How to feed and care for your new baby.

ISBN 978-0-9701245-6-2
$12.95

**Also available in Spanish.
To order, call (800) 434-4633 or visit www.iha4health.org.**

# Other Books in the Series

ISBN 978-0-9701245-4-8
$12.95

## What To Do For Senior Health*

There are many things that you can do to take charge of your health during your senior years. This book tells about:

- Body changes that come with aging.
- Common health problems of seniors.
- Things to consider about health insurance.
- How to choose a doctor and where to get health care.
- Buying and taking medicines.
- Simple things you can do to prevent falls and accidents.
- What you can do to stay healthy.

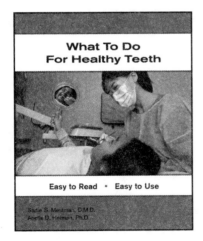

ISBN 978-0-9721048-0-9
$12.95

## What To Do For Healthy Teeth

It is important to take good care of your teeth from an early age. This book tells how to do that. It also explains all about teeth, gums, and how dentists work with you to keep your teeth healthy.

- How to care for your teeth and gums.
- What you need to care for your teeth and gums.
- Caring for your teeth when you're having a baby.
- Caring for your child's teeth.
- When to call the dentist.
- What to expect at a dental visit.
- Dental care needs for seniors.
- What to do if you hurt your mouth or teeth.

Also available in Spanish.
*Also available in Vietnamese.
To order, call (800) 434-4633 or visit www.iha4health.org.

# Other Books in the Series

ISBN 978-0-9721048-4-7
$12.95

## What To Do When Your Child Is Heavy

There are many things you can do to help your heavy child live a healthy lifestyle. Here's an easy to read, easy to use book that tells you:

- How to tell if your child is heavy.
- How to shop and pay for healthy food.
- Dealing with your heavy child's feelings and self-esteem.
- How to read the Nutrition Facts Label.
- Healthy breakfasts, lunches and dinners.
- Correct portion sizes.
- Why exercise is so important.
- Tips for eating healthy when you eat out.
- Information on diabetes and other health problems of heavy children.

ISBN 978-0-9720148-6-1
$12.95

## What To Do When Your Child Has Asthma

Having a child with asthma can be scary. This easy to read, easy to use book tells you what you can do to help your child deal with asthma:

- How to tell if your child needs help right away.
- Signs that your child has asthma.
- Triggers for an asthma attack.
- Putting together an Asthma Action Plan.
- How to use a peak flow meter.
- The different kinds of asthma medicine.
- How to talk to your child's day care and teachers about your child's asthma.
- Making sure your child gets enough exercise.
- Helping your child to take their asthma medicine the right way.
- What to do for problems such as upset stomach, hay fever and stuffy nose.

Also available in Spanish.
To order, call (800) 434-4633 or visit www.iha4health.org.